Mid-life Magic

Designing the next chapter of your life

— Lorraine

Lorraine Clemes

Mid-life Magic: Designing the next chapter of your life

Order this book online at www.trafford.com
or email orders@trafford.com

Most Trafford titles are also available at major online book retailers.

© Copyright 2009 Lorraine Dawn Clemes.
All rights reserved. No part of this publication may be reproduced, stored in a retrieval system, or transmitted, in any form or by any means, electronic, mechanical, photocopying, recording, or otherwise, without the written prior permission of the author.

Production Credits
Book and cover design: Roy Diment, Vivencia Resources Group
Author photo: Thea Menagh @ www.AFittingImage.com
Cover image: Wendell Franks /iStockphoto

Note for Librarians: A cataloguing record for this book is available from Library and Archives Canada at www.collectionscanada.ca/amicus/index-e.html

Printed in Victoria, BC, Canada.

ISBN: 9781-4251-879-9-6

Careers / Retirement / Personal Growth

We at Trafford believe that it is the responsibility of us all, as both individuals and corporations, to make choices that are environmentally and socially sound. You, in turn, are supporting this responsible conduct each time you purchase a Trafford book, or make use of our publishing services. To find out how you are helping, please visit www.trafford.com/responsiblepublishing.html

Our mission is to efficiently provide the world's finest, most comprehensive book publishing service, enabling every author to experience success. To find out how to publish your book, your way, and have it available worldwide, visit us online at www.trafford.com

Trafford PUBLISHING® www.trafford.com

North America & international
toll-free: 1 888 232 4444 (USA & Canada)
phone: 250 383 6864 ♦ fax: 250 383 6804 ♦ email: info@trafford.com

The United Kingdom & Europe
phone: +44 (0)1865 487 395 ♦ local rate: 0845 230 9601
facsimile: +44 (0)1865 481 507 ♦ email: info.uk@trafford.com

*With thanks to my grandmother
Annie Alma Schell McCormack (1889-1979)
who wrote this to me in my childhood*

*Learn to make the most of life,
make glad each passing day,
for life will never bring you back
the chances swept away.*

Acknowledgements

Writing a book takes time and focus. I want to acknowledge the many people who have accompanied me along the way. A small group of us met in the context of our graduate education and have remained friends. Professionally we studied leadership with a focus on the individual. Our interest was in how leaders remain true to both themselves and their organizations. Each of us has succeeded in dreaming large in our own lives and we continue to inspire and support each other. Thank you to Doug Berquist, Gillian Johnston and Christine Stanger for your ongoing encouragement, reality checks and fun reunions.

Margie Hart and Linda Mitz Sadiq were the first of my friends and colleagues to see and react to my conceived framework. Their thoughtful comments and ongoing interest were invaluable.

Galina Coffey-Lewis was there when I printed out the first draft which she read with care. I value her reactions, advice, and friendship.

I threw out a wide net in researching and naming the book and had helpful discussions with friends in Canada, the United States and Australia. Thanks to Don and Wanda Allen, Mary Ann Archer, Brenda Carrigan, Laura Carrigan Clemes and Robert Clemes,

Chantalle Fish, Irene and Peter Gardiner-Harding, Susan Graham, Sue Griggs, Garry and Pat Lander, Allan and Susan Lappin, Jim Lewis, Carol MacKinnon, Janet Matts, Allan O'Marra, Eileen Page, Pat and Jordan Pearl, Ahsan Sadiq, Lyz Sayer, Ajay and Tammara Sirsi, Christine Turner, Tony Wilson, Janet Evans Woodbridge, Barb and John Woodruffe and Susan Wright.

I'm fortunate to have sons, both excellent writers, who provided feedback and support. Thanks David and Ryan Treleaven. I'd also like to thank Isabel Elliott McCormack, my aunt, who continually asked with encouragement "how's the book coming?" Other friends who showed ongoing interest were Vera Arajs, Patricia McDowell and Heather Sperdakos.

I work with people as they create exciting, sometimes magical scenarios in their lives and I wanted to use their cases to show you what's possible. Thanks to the friends and colleagues who allowed me to share their actual experiences. For confidentiality we changed their names. There are a few examples that are composites of clients, representative of the types of situations that I've commonly encountered over the years. None of these cases contain references to any one specific individual. Where I refer to my own life or use the pronoun "our" to identify with the generation in mid-life, I've done so in the spirit of Jack Kornfield's observations that it is through our personal experience that we make sense of our world.[1]

Introduction

When I read a book I like to know why an author is drawn to the topic. I'll start there. As far back as I can remember I framed life as a journey. I know it sounds like a cliché but I remember visualizing it that way at a young age. I moved frequently as a child so feeling sad at what I was leaving, imagining what was coming next, adapting, making new friends, and keeping in touch with special old ones became second nature. My parents were skilled at providing a predictable base in the home and supporting me in venturing into the community to find where I fit. My awareness of life being full of surprises, choices, and opportunities started early. I've always been interested in how people discover who they are and how they make important life decisions.

I named my company Life Design Consultants with the view that life is most rewarding if we're intentional and proactive about our decisions and if we acknowledge what matters to us and head in that direction. I work with successful people of all ages who want to discover what they really want to be when they grow up. When someone loses their job, or becomes depressed in their career, or their plan to leave full-time work at a specific age changes due to an economic downturn, they may feel scared and lost.

I learned ways to be in, and move beyond that fearful place in my own mid-life adventure, in my professional work as a career consultant, executive and life coach and from friends and colleagues. I see myself as a facilitator. I'm optimistic yet practical. I'll give you information and encouragement as well as cautions and hints. I've seen people thrive through change, and others get stuck. I've experienced both extremes myself. I'm sharing a seven-step approach that works.

The steps will work with people of any age looking to design the next stage of their life. It's especially relevant at mid-life. By then we realize that even well-planned routes have detours, some choices we make close doors and that serendipity is part of life's story. What is the magic then at mid-life? It's the opportunity to respect your tested skills, experiences and self-awareness and toss them into the pot, make it sizzle by adding your dreams and use the impetus of fleeting time as a catalyst to move forward.

I've made the book interactive so that you can make progress in your situation and included information that is most relevant for people in mid-life looking forward. I vacillated about whether to use the word *retirement*. I decided to do so while being clear that it is a word and concept that, in the way we have known it, has expired. There isn't yet a replacement word, and with the diversity and creativity of upcoming generations' lifestyle choices, there may never be.

My specific interest in how the concept of retirement would change began over a decade ago. Since then I've clipped and downloaded articles, attended conferences, done a doctoral study, noted the statistics and most importantly engaged in deep dialogue on the topic with my network. The purpose of my next life stage includes participating in this societal shift and reframing what is possible and desirable in these years for individuals and our world.

The focus of this book is your personal possibilities and journey, but choices are made in the context of our times. In the 1960s and 1970s, people now turning 60 were part of a social movement for liberalization and increased individuality. "Baby boomers" or "boomers" are terms that refer to the increase in population that occurred after World War II ended when there was a sustained increase in births in many countries. Boomer refers to those born between 1947 and 1966 in Canada and 1946 and 1964 in the United States.[1] In the 1980s and 1990s, mergers, downsizing, flattening of organizations, outsourcing, globalization, and technology impacted our career paths challenging predictability, and increasing our responsibility for our choices. These changes impacted our lives.

I came of age when options were expanding due to such things as increased access to higher education and birth control. This was especially true for women. I've lived my adult life conscious of the lack of role models to show ways to walk through the doors that we pried open. The good news is that this has presented us opportunities to be creative in pioneering new possibilities. This will not stop as we move through mid-life.

Retirement is not what it used to be. It's often more like a lifestyle transition. Today people who decide to retire often still work, go back to school, start a new career or an entrepreneurial venture, volunteer overseas, or travel for adventure. People are doing diverse things during this ever-expanding life stage of mid-life and beyond. While in the final stages of writing this book in the fall of 2008, a global economic crisis impacted many people's retirement plans. This makes the type of process I'm suggesting, and being intentional about your choices, even more relevant and important.

The impact of our choices will be immense. There are so many of us. In the 2006 census there were over 10 million people between ages 40 and 60 in Canada; so over the next couple of decades almost a third of Canada's population will be what used to be called retirement age.[2]

I started writing this book by asking what I'd learned personally and professionally that I could share to help people live their lives most fully. Most people don't *really* believe that their deepest dreams can come true. I know this is so because I frequently encounter this belief with clients. I'll show you how to change and move towards appreciating the opportunities you have through your choices. Writing this book, trusting that it will be helpful and empowering for you, is a choice I made with integrity and intentionality. Whatever age you are, you have less time today than you did yesterday to find what matters most to you.

My hope is that my book helps you to become clear on what the next chapter of your life can be and how you can attain your dreams.

Contents

Acknowledgements — v
Introduction — vii

Part One
Getting Started

1. Overview
   Seven steps to designing your future — 3
2. Components of Well-being
   Not just a life – but a fulfilling life — 9
3. Pioneering Possibilities
   Reinventing retirement — 23

Part Two
Creating Your Options

4. Reviewing and Dreaming
   Looking backwards and forwards — 45
5. Creating Potential Options
   Customizing your future — 73
6. Researching, Reality Checking and Planning
   Spiraling towards clarity — 95

Part Three
Making it Happen

7. Overcoming Challenges
   Avoiding pitfalls and transitioning well   111

8. Living Your Dream
   If not now — then when?   127

Notes   131

Additional Resources   139

Index

About the Author

Part One

Getting Started

Chapter 1

Overview

Seven steps to designing your future

People expect to have strong voices in their work and life choices these days. Especially as we mature we're less inclined towards activities or relationships that don't fit with what's important to us. Is this true for you?

Discovering and living according to our values is empowering. The way that happens can change at different ages and stages of our lives. People initiating change do best by developing a strategy that inspires them and respects what they care about most. There's an art in this strategy to achieving a balance between envisaging possibility while remaining realistic. I believe that both aspects are needed. I'll lead you through seven steps that provide structure for those who prefer a framework. If that feels restrictive to you, then use the activities and information I provide as a guide to give you what you need.

How the book is organized

Part One: Getting Started

The *Overview* explains how the book is organized and illustrates the process we'll be using.

STEP ONE looks at the building blocks of a fulfilling life, or what I call *Components of Well-being*. You'll consider the components and how they relate to your life and assess your profile so that you can include what you discover in your planning.

Individuals now aged 40 and older are *Pioneering Possibilities* at mid-life or retirement and this chapter is for people who want to understand how and why "this is not your parent's retirement."

Part Two: Creating Your Options

STEP TWO profiles your personal circumstances by *Reviewing* your life. There's valuable information in the patterns and themes that are uniquely yours; and they offer clues on how you can get satisfaction in your next life chapter. I've included questions and activities to get you to mine your past in order to create your best options for the future.

We'll look forward in STEP THREE and you'll do some *Dreaming*. There are important questions to consider, suggestions and activities that will get at what's important to you for your ideal future.

We'll integrate the information you've uncovered from the well-being, reviewing and dreaming activities to help you in STEP FOUR which looks at *Creating Potential Options*.

Next I'll give you suggestions to consider in STEP FIVE through *Researching, Reality Checking and Planning* your possibilities.

Part Three: Making it Happen

We'll explore *Overcoming Challenges* in STEP SIX. In this step we'll consider common challenges that you may encounter in implementing your plan and living through the changes. I'll share hints for handling the challenges and transitions that enable you to be successful on your own terms.

STEP SEVEN is my invitation to consider working towards living your fullest life right now – *Living Your Dream*. If you've picked up this book it may be because you or someone you love is struggling to know how or where to initiate change. By the last chapter you'll have asked yourself important questions and explored several possibilities in order to decide which option works best for you.

As you work along, I invite you to embrace the optimism of your youth and integrate it with the insight of your years to create your next steps. To target achievement of what matters to you listen to your intuition, acknowledge your maturity, strengths and resources. We're most powerful when we align what we do with who we are. That's why it's so important to become clear about your preferences and dreams.

You may be unhappy in your current life, may need to readjust your retirement plans or may already be proactive about your future. Whether you're looking to rebalance, renew or reinvent a meaningful life, this process can help you.

Suggestions for using the book

I read a book like this with a highlighter in hand noting what resonates with me. As an educator I know that other approaches work too:
- get a journal, or allot a computer file to record your insights, memorable points and things you want to reflect on more fully
- write in the margins, talk back to me if you disagree, and make the book something you can refer back to and react to
- read it concurrently with a friend or colleague with whom you can share your reactions and ideas
- form a small group to explore this; meet over time or set aside a weekend and go somewhere with good food, places to walk outside and be more reflective than you might normally be; take turns being the client in working through the activities
- use what you discover in reading the book to open a dialogue with your spouse or friends
- bring your own style to how you use the process – you're in charge!

If you want a life that honors yet stretches you, and you're wondering "now what?" then this book is for you. It's meant to involve you and support your continued success. Be honest, and notice what resonates with you. The world needs you fully engaged. The approach illustrated on the next page is sound, so use it to consider and plan your next steps. Make it work. Enjoy!

Living Your Dream
↑
Overcoming Challenges
↑
Researching
Reality Checking
Planning
↑ ↑
Creating Potential Options
↗ ↑ ↖
Components   Reviewing   Dreaming
of
Well-being

Chapter 2

Components of Well-being

Not just a life – but a fulfilling life

*The degree to which we invest in our well-being
forms the base on which we build our life.
A narrow focus or ignored components
yield a less resilient structure.
A firm, broad foundation supports the towers
reaching to your dreams.*

This book is about creating your version of thriving, not just surviving in your life. Incorporating components of well-being into your plan can maximize your experience. Well-being considers the whole person and involves a way of life oriented towards optimal health in which the individual's body, mind, and spirit are integrated resulting in a fuller life. What constitutes a meaningful life for you? Deciding this is STEP ONE.

It's a personal question, and only you can make decisions for your own situation. Lest you skip over this chapter too quickly, consider how important it is to invest in your well-being. Statistically we're living longer and the strain on available societal resources of that increased longevity and a proportionally larger aging population is a wake-up call that challenges us each to be responsible for our health. Ken Dychtwald, a leader in the field of aging says that after nearly 30 years of intense involvement in this field he fears that our avoidance of critical age-related issues could lead to numerous personal and social disasters down the road.[1] The challenge is both societal and personal. It's the latter over which you have the most control.

My relationship with well-being

In my teens my interest in understanding why some people exude positive energy while others dispense negativity took me to the library. It's why I studied psychology in university and adult renewal and transformation with Frederic Hudson at The Hudson Institute of Santa Barbara.[2]

I've been conscious of issues of wellness and balance since my last year of high school. It was a marvelous year. I was on committees, studying hard, partying and dating, and working evenings and weekends to save money for university. I put my energy so fully into so many things that I was diagnosed with exhaustion when I literally couldn't get out of bed. It was frightening at the time although it was a gift for me to have experienced the consequences of getting so out of balance early in life.

By the time I'd married, had children and returned to my career, managing priorities and finding balance again became a challenge. In addition to working in a career that I loved, I was a wife and mother and did part-time graduate studies. It took lots of planning and energy and after a few years I started to get physical symptoms of overload. I decided to learn about the mind-body connection. As luck would have it, a woman experienced in meditation joined my department, and has been a mentor and friend to this day. This highlights something I believe. When you get clear about your intent, stay open to synchronicity as opportunities often come your way.

While facilitating stress management workshops at a corporate leadership center, I was struck by how little managers knew of the link between their behavior, stress and illness. I wondered why we weren't taught coping skills earlier in life. So I independently researched and developed guided visualization and stress management audio-programs for children and teens. I produced *A Special Place: Self-Esteem & Relaxation Techniques for Children*, and *Time-Out: Problem-solving & Stress Management for Teenagers*, which are downloadable from my website.[3] A pediatric oncologist wrote me years later that she used the guided visualization program with some of her young patients during their chemotherapy treatments to decrease their discomfort. This touched me deeply and reinforced my interest in studying holistic approaches.

My view of well-being includes the interconnection of mind, body and spirit. At an integrative medicine workshop I attended with Dr. Andrew Weil, a Harvard trained M.D., medical doctors and other healing professionals from across North America shared ways they're combining eastern and western approaches into their medical practices.[4]

As I broaden my experience I frame well-being as related to energy flow. Scientists studying quantum physics have shown that we are all energy, or organized atoms.[5] Our body is not as solid as science once believed – we "are" energy. This is relevant for choices we make about our health and our interactions with people. Proximity to some people makes us feel revived. Some have just the opposite effect. Your body is giving you feedback and you can include this information to make important decisions in your life.

You do this by becoming aware of your own positive or negative energetic shifts. A trained eye sees and feels the changed energy externally, and you can become aware of the different feelings within yourself. In my psychology internship I was taught to watch for physical evidence when a client shows their passion for something. They get a sparkle in their eyes and their breathing rate, pace of speech, skin color and body language change. Energetically they are different, more alive. When does that happen for you?

Remember my high school experience? I still don't always hear the earliest warning whispers from my body. However, I respect the need to keep my energy centers open and create opportunities to check-in with myself and rebalance when I become aware of problems. It's not always comfortable to feel what my body has to say, but I act more authentically and make better decisions when I do.

There are numerous books on strategies for maximizing health and longevity, which are beyond the scope of this book. You may refer to them as part of your research activities. I've included some that I've read in the Additional Resources section.[6] Here are components that contribute to well-being:
Achievement
Authenticity
Intimacy, emotional health
Learning, growth, openness to new experiences
Meaning, life purpose, legacy
Mental, cognitive
Physical
Pleasure, enjoyment
Social connection, community
Spiritual, belief system

Achievement

Achievement means setting and reaching goals that matter to you. It may be reaching a level of responsibility in your career, or developing skills in a sport, a hobby, or a life role. It may be attaining improved health status by doing such things as quitting smoking or exercising regularly.

Some people focus on visible achievements. Some are more private but just as achievement oriented. What achievements do you value most? As you go through life, ask yourself if you're at peace with what you've achieved. Can you accept your limitations and plan for remaining aspirations?

Authenticity

Authenticity refers to your ability to be yourself fully and deeply in your actions and when relating to others. It means that you acknowledge your weaknesses as well as your strengths and are able to make decisions based on that recognition. It means being honest with what is present, rather than worrying about the future, or regretting the past. To be authentic is to be in touch with your inner thoughts and feelings and act on them. You "walk your talk."

Intimacy, emotional health

Intimacy means being able and willing to share ourselves deeply and maintain trust through the difficult as well as easy times. Emotional health implies that you're aware of and have a vocabulary for your feelings and you have the ability to communicate them and to receive feedback non-defensively. It means that you're able to maintain long-term commitments and relationships with family, friends, and others who matter in your life.

There's a difference between spending time with someone with whom you have common interests, which I call "social connection", and intimacy. Especially as we age and people pass through and out of our lives, investing in true dialogue and intimacy contributes to closure and emotional well-being.

Learning, growth, openness to new experiences

This component refers to learning new things, broadening your perspective and being comfortable with change. It means keeping up with the times and stretching to seek growth experiences. It could be learning a new technique in order to become proficient in an activity, or in your profession, learning a new language in order to travel or keeping mentally agile. The possibilities are endless. Discover your ideal balance between being comfortable and seeking new experiences.

How do you learn best? In formal settings with credentialed teachers, by trial and error, informally through watching educational television, reading or by engaging in self-study at your own pace? Moving to a new community or changing jobs presents opportunities to expand your vantage point. Whether acquiring a new skill, developing emotional resilience, exploring spirituality, or adapting to a health challenge, learning can improve the quality of our lives. In his seventies, my dad learned how to type and use a computer so he could stay in touch with his grandchildren away at university. Dr. Allen Tough, social scientist, educator and futurist who writes extensively on informal adult learning calls these "adult learning projects."[7]

Meaning, life purpose, legacy

We function best when our life has meaning to us. Living life with purpose can keep us healthy. Being healthy allows us to have richer experiences with the people we love and contribute our skills for the betterment of our community in whatever scale possible and personally desirable. I'd invite you to think about this and consider it in your plan. Lily Tomlin said: "All my life, I always wanted to be somebody. Now I see that I should have been more specific." Are you engaged in using your gifts and passions? Beyond mid-life you may start to reflect on your legacy and whether your footprint matters. What will you be remembered for? In what way will you leave the world a better place?

Mental, cognitive

This refers to our ability to use rational, logical thought processes. "Use it, or lose it" seems true regarding our mental capabilities. Research indicates that the brain has a remarkable and enduring capacity to make new connections, absorb new data and acquire new skills. Studies show that memory is improved by keeping mentally active. Activities such as doing crosswords, learning a new language, memorizing and doing something novel contribute to cognitive health. Other ways to keep mentally stimulated are participating in lively conversations, complex problem solving, listening to intellectually based radio or television, keeping up to date with current events or investing, taking courses, starting a hobby or learning how to use a new technology.

Physical

Physical well-being means keeping our body healthy through nutrition, exercise, not smoking, maintaining a healthy weight and taking other preventative measures to maximize how well it functions. Our use and abuse of it, plus our genetic predisposition, start to catch up with us by mid-life. We may encounter changes in our physical health with such chronic diseases as diabetes, heart attacks, cancers, arthritis, or deficiencies such as hearing loss and decreasing vigor.

In addition to traditional medicine, people are increasingly integrating preventative activities and natural healing approaches. Many healing activities address the energy flow in our bodies and allow our body to repair and our presence to be strong. Some examples of such activities are: acupuncture, aikido, breathwork, cranial sacral, guided visualization, homeopathy, meditation, pilates, qigong, tai chi, tantric activities and yoga.

Pleasure, enjoyment

Allowing pleasure into our lives contributes to our well-being; yet it is something that challenges people. Things that people say bring them pleasure include being creative, laughing, being in nature, dancing, reading, playing a sport, sharing time with friends, traveling to new places and playing with a child or pet.

Leisure is a form of pleasure for some. Reiner defines leisure as activities that are freely chosen, provide satisfaction, a sense of commitment, arouse interest and provide pleasure. She found that people who get overly involved in competitive activities, and whose main motivation is winning, risk crossing back into work, not leisure mode.[8] Rollins' research shows that "people who consistently fail to incorporate leisure into their lives are more likely to feel depressed, disconnected and dissatisfied."[9] As George Bernard Shaw said: "We don't stop playing because we grow old; we grow old because we stop playing."

Social connection, community

This component relates to feeling connected to something or someone outside yourself and having sufficient social skills to attract and maintain relationships. Community is the sense of being associated with others around a value, activity or cause. Many who work in organizations take strength from their identity with these communities. What will the impact be when they are no longer in that role or organization? Some people may face a significant and perhaps surprising sense of loss when that community is no longer there for them. Might that be true for you?

As a career transition consultant, I always asked what my clients expected they would miss most about their job. Often it was the people. Men and women frequently became emotional in response to that question. You may just like to have people around you, and to participate in groups. Some people just need to fill their time in a way that doesn't make them feel isolated and others genuinely thrive in interaction and connection. What role does social connection play in your life?

Spiritual, belief system

Have you developed a perspective on the meaning of life, your sense of place in the universe, and the reality of impermanence? The issue is that you've taken the time in your life to consider this and are seeking or are at peace with your belief.

By mid-life we've usually experienced the paradoxes of life and loss. We're often in touch with something larger than ourselves. Some people keep busy and focused only on the external world. The spiritual component speaks to our ability to also turn inward and discover our answers to questions of life and death so that we're able to let go of our ego and eventually, life.

Death. How do you react to that word? Do you let yourself react to it? Where do you feel your reaction? In your head, or your heart? I include death as an element of well-being because the earlier in life we accept our mortality, the more we can let go of fear and have the energy to embrace life and really live.

Dr. Viktor Frankl, a holocaust survivor who wrote extensively about the meaning of life, suggested that spirituality forms the essence of humanity.[10] There are many practices that people engage in that provide the opportunity to explore these issues. Some find this within organized religion, others by reading, attending workshops or retreats, being creative or appreciating artistic offerings, in practices such as meditation, breathwork or in being outdoors. Here is one definition of spirituality:

Spirituality is an on-going journey characterized by an intense, consuming motivation to "become", and by which we elicit transformative experiences of ourselves and the world. It is characterized by an increased emphasis on how we experience ourselves in the world, and how we experience our integration and connection to the world. It is ultimately, the force by which we come to know our true nature. To the extent that we recognize this force, remain open to its possibilities and nurture it with our daily activities – we are spiritual beings.[11]

Considerations

- The Cornell Retirement and Well-being Study (2000) found that well-being is related to willingness to renegotiate roles, having something to wake up for, social support, a high level of physical and mental activity, a strong financial plan and a healthy spouse; skills that were linked to health were the ability to accentuate the positive, accept yourself as you are, be in the moment, help others, plan for pleasure, maintain an internal locus of control, laugh and smile, sense of wonder about the world and gratefulness for what you have.[12]

- Integrating aspects of several components that matter most to you into your future plans is an effective way to keep in balance.

- Over time the priorities and balance among the components may change, by design or changed circumstances, so be ready to reassess and be adaptable.

- Life-skills such as our ability to be realistic, resilient and attain support for ourselves, adapt to change, cope with loss and surrender control become increasingly important as we age; so if these are not strengths of yours, you may want to consider targeting growth in that area and make it a step in your plan.

- In Freidan's study of vital men and women in their 70s and 80s the common themes that emerged were that they felt they had choice and purpose in their lives including continuing their careers if they wanted or being active in the community; they demonstrated qualities of trust, risk-taking, adaptability, non-conformity and the ability to live in the present, experience growth, change and aliveness.[13]

Activities

To assess your well-being profile, ask yourself these questions:

Which of the above components of a well-balanced lifestyle do you currently invest the most time in?

Which components are missing for you, or could be more fully explored?

Which ones do you enjoy the most?

Intuitively, what do you need more and less of?

Is there an area where you'd benefit from getting professional support?

What's your personal story of well-being and balance in your life and how can you apply what you know about yourself in designing your future?

Rank the 10 components by indicating how satisfied you are with taking that component "as is" into your next stage.
1 (most) 10 (least)

    ___ Achievement
    ___ Authenticity
    ___ Intimacy, emotional health
    ___ Learning, growth, openness to new experiences
    ___ Meaning, life purpose, legacy
    ___ Mental, cognitive
    ___ Physical
    ___ Pleasure, enjoyment
    ___ Social connection, community
    ___ Spiritual, belief system

For each component what specifically do you need to:

start doing?
continue doing?
do more of?
stop doing?

What or who:
depletes your energy?
supports your efforts at achieving well-being and balance?

Now capture the observations that you've made about your own profile as you worked through this chapter and keep them in mind as you create your options.

Chapter 3

Pioneering Possibilities

Reinventing retirement

*This is not our parent's retirement.
Our life circumstances and workplaces are
more diversified and dynamic.
We have the opportunity to create new
patterns and possibilities.*

Over a decade ago I decided to follow my hunch that retirement would be different for the next generation and undertook doctoral research on that topic. It was novel at the time to consider that the concept of retirement would change for future generations. That time has passed.

As each generation enters the stream of history, the lives of its members are marked by societal events, and in time they leave their own imprint. If you're interested in how and why retirement is changing for the next generation, then you may benefit from reading this chapter.

You may only be 40 but be a planner and want to create a long-term plan for yourself; or you may have left your career years ago and want to do something in the workplace again.

I'm including information in this chapter that is most pertinent for those whose next step is to design their retirement. For most of us, by choice or circumstance, the role models of previous generations will not serve us well. The world has changed and so have we. If this isn't of interest to you, or you want to focus only on your personal process, then you may decide to skip this chapter and proceed to the rest of the book.

The men and women I interviewed said that the word *retired* evokes an image of being inactive and out of date, impending old age, and lacking a meaningful role in society. They preferred to talk about winding down, shifting gears and often reinventing themselves. This life stage is being seen and marketed as a new beginning offering increased freedom and opportunity. Women, especially, mentioned that with increased longevity they expect to spend up to a third of their lives in the phase traditionally called retirement. That's a career in itself.

There are some who still view that stage with the lens of their parents and head to a gated retirement community at 55. They're not the pioneers of this generation. And it's the pioneers who open the way for those who follow. The terms that people in my study suggested to describe the new retirement were: rebalance, renewal, reinvent, redirect, refocus, reframe and transition. What word would you use to capture what you'd like this life stage to be for you?

History of retirement

During my graduate work I undertook a comprehensive investigation of studies in the history, definition and impact of retirement. I found that early research was flawed by virtue of the data used and the focus was often on leisure activities and roles. Until recently women were studied only in a gendered model in relation to her role in the family and as a subset of men's retirement.[1] For reasons I discuss in this chapter retirement is an increasingly complex and evolving concept.

Stereotypically, in generations who came of age before the late 1960s, the wage earner of a family, typically the man, left long-term employment at 65, if he lived that long, and headed off for his reward for years of working. The woman, whose work had usually been raising children and taking care of the household, followed along. Often his dream was touring the country in an RV, going south in the winters or relocating to a small town. This didn't apply to everyone. Single women were often not eligible for company pensions.

The earliest boomers were rewarded for conformity in their youth, but they fought for and changed rules over time. Those who came of age in the late 1960s and 1970s didn't want to fit into the silos of the past and wanted more say and less structure. Birth control options expanded, couples lived together without marrying, drinking ages and voting ages were lowered, and women started to enter professions and non-traditional jobs. The Vietnam War, campus unrest, political assassinations in the United States and a lowered voting age rallied us. "Trudeaumania" was the name given in 1968 to the impact of Pierre Trudeau. He was a nonconformist politician who entered the stage, became Prime Minster of Canada and engaged us with momentum for a more liberal vision. Increasing numbers of men and women acquired post secondary education. There was extensive change.

Evidence of that change was captured by Gail Sheehy in her book *New Passages* where she explored the revolution of the boomer's adult life cycle in a large study. She focused on the years past 45, which she called the infancy of our "second adulthood." She noted that the individual psychological journey is tightly entwined with the social context in which we develop. As there were significant changes in society and the workplace throughout the adult years of the boomers, why would we be surprised that our expectations and dreams for retirement would also be impacted? Currently, boomers are in their early 40s through to early 60s. Due to our large numbers the impact of this cohort has been felt at each life stage.

Why retirement is changing

The reasons why most of us will not retire in the traditional way can be explained by looking at what has changed over our lifetime. It includes aspects about men and women as individuals, their family lives, the workplace available to them and trends in society. Specifically:

- *Men and women are living longer* Statistics Canada states that the life expectancy for men born in 1920 was 59 and for women, 61 years. For men born in

1950, the life expectancy had risen to age 66 and for women, to 71. By 1993 the life expectancy was 75 years for men and 81 years for women. Dr. Kenneth Manton, a demographer at Duke University, predicts that a woman who reaches the age of 50, free of cancer and heart disease, can expect to see her 92nd birthday.[2]

Broadcast journalist Walter Cronkite was quoted at age 87 as saying it was a "gross mistake" to have retired at 65 – "I didn't know I'd be healthy for so long."[3]

- *Increased career opportunities for women* Earliest boomer women were a generation socialized to be "traditional" women but were then influenced by the women's movement to consider different possibilities for themselves. Professional women in particular consider themselves pioneers as they were often the first women in their families to earn degrees and combine careers and parenting. Many had a transformative vision, a dream and expectation of changing society and the workplace through their individual and collective efforts. Women were strongly motivated by this and have impacted the world outside of the home. They're used to being the first of their gender to attempt or achieve something.

  Seventy percent of the women in one study of senior executive women indicated that they have had no role models and they believe that they will always do life differently from previous generations of women.[4] Their view extends to their concept of their own retirement. When I researched studies on women and retirement for my thesis, data were either not collected for women or their husbands were asked to speak for them.[5]

- *There's increased diversity within the current generation at mid-life* Dual earner professional couples evolved lifestyles quite different from their parents' generation or from those earning minimum wage or with one earner in the family. Kathleen Brehony, a clinical psychologist, found that "In fact there has never been a generation that has so many differences among its members."[6]
Diversity includes people who are divorced, choosing-to-be singles, dual career earners, single parents, and adults who are parents to young children when in their fifties. Freidan explored a broad sampling of ordinary men and women, then 50 years of age and older, and found an increasing diversity in life patterns and less predictability in our personal and workplace lives.[7]

- *Family structure diversity and increased divorce in society* has meant that many approach their 60s with second families, children still to support through university, spousal and support payments, and considerations of where to live so as to be accessible for co-parenting responsibilities. A widened definition of what constitutes a couple or family and more divorces and common law arrangements, shared custody of children, single parents and postponed parenthood and blended families can impact retirement decisions. I know couples in second marriages who are concurrently parents of teenagers and grandparents of a first family.

- *Workplace changes* over the past twenty years mean that long-term, uninterrupted, full-time employment is rare. Mergers, the impact of technology, globalization and flattening of organizations, and especially a decrease in middle management have meant that long service and resultant retirement pensions have disappeared as an option for many. Technology or outsourcing to other countries displaced many people's jobs. The trend of hiring part-time or contract workers rather than full-time employees again has changed retirement realities and opportunities. Due to these changes there also are more options than to work or not work.

- *Discontinuous careers* for men and women due to restructuring and mass downsizing of organizations means decisions about our futures may include working longer in order to accumulate sufficient financial resources. Those who interrupted their careers to upgrade their education, or shifted into a new career when their jobs became lost or redundant may plan to continue to work longer. Eichler found that family life tends to have a negative effect on a woman's economic position in part because if a couple divorces the single most important asset today is access to job-related benefits including earnings, pensions and health benefits.

Women may not have these benefits if they have had a discontinuous work pattern in order to accommodate family needs. This work pattern and fewer pensions lead to more uncertainty regarding financial considerations for retirement.[8]

- *Defining work broadly* impacts how we view our activity as we age. Meaning doesn't come just from working for money. Sense of purpose means that your life has personal meaning and that you're contributing to something that you value. Not all women who are now in mid-life worked for money outside the home. Griggs and Wright defined work as "any meaningful task that contributes to the well-being either of self or others, and requires some skill to perform. Work can be volunteering. It can be education. It can be homemaking, it can be writing one's memoirs."[9] The professional women in my study who worked inside the home while their children were young accomplished things such as starting a co-operative nursery and organizing a women's shelter. Another woman left employment to work for several years attending graduate school.

- *Individuals created new career opportunities for themselves* through self-employment, combining part-time work and retraining or upgrading, consulting in their area of expertise or becoming entrepreneurs. Several individuals in my study and particularly women in professions such as law created options that allowed them independence within their own practices where there was more freedom to set hours, work part-time, focus their work and arrange sabbaticals. Those who built their careers on that framework already have transition options in place. One man I know leveraged his volunteer work into a second career that lasted decades when his previous role was eliminated.

- *Financial realities* include job loss for some and the decrease of people's retirement funds when global economic markets readjusted and large losses were incurred in 2008. With large numbers of people approaching 60, and self-funding retirement being so prevalent for this demographic, many people may choose to continue to earn money for more years to make up the losses incurred.

The above issues will financially and emotionally impact what is possible and desirable in our futures. We're living with the impact of these patterns and the story is just beginning to be written.

How retirement is changing

Canadians aged 55-64 have become the fastest growing demographic in the country.[10] The oldest boomers in Canada turned 60 in 2007. Many of this generation and those to follow are reluctant or financially unable to retire in the traditional way. Many see retirement as a process of continuing or rejuvenating their lives and eventually winding down. They feel positive about their emerging version of retirement. The components that became apparent as important in my research were that there was a sense of purpose, growth and learning, and meaningful connection to others.

Retirement used to mean when someone who had been employed full-time ceased to work for money. I encounter people who say they are retired, yet they work for money and are contributing in active and important ways in their community and have no plans to stop. Others start and stop career activities for long periods and intersperse travel or education with earning money. In the interim periods, are they retired? The following lists describe elements of the two extremes of retirement, with many patterns emerging in a continuum between the two:

Traditional retirement
- stopping paid work
- mainly involved in leisure, travel, hobbies
- volunteer work, boards
- a mind-set of being out of the mainstream
- a "then-and-now" demarcation

Pioneers – the evolving meaning of retirement
- beginning in a new career area or role for yourself
- gradually decreasing activity in the same career field or job
- significant involvement in a cause that's important to you
- leadership or other involvement in volunteer or international work
- transformation, radical change that is often values oriented

- consulting, projects, series of contracts
- full-time or part-time, maybe for a long time, seasonal work
- mini-transitions, blurred lines between working and not
- re-education
- combining work and play

- *Demographic patterns* of North America present a future situation where there will be increasing shortages of workers due to a decreasing population of younger generations. Organizations will be challenged to find ways to attract and keep the best workers, and succession management and retention will be an issue as people give up full-time work over the next few decades. Shortages will be especially true for places like government, teaching, healthcare and professions where there is a pension or retirement allowance. It also means expertise related to such things as our public safety and medical care may be in short supply. This is an area that has serious implications in society requiring prompt attention beyond the scope of this book. However, concurrent with the numerous downsides, this reality may open up opportunities for new and continuing forms of career longevity and work arrangements.

- *Common career patterns* that have emerged over the past decades include mixtures of contracts, entrepreneurship, part-time work and shorter periods of employment with one organization. A Statistics Canada survey found that most managers and professionals who are self-employed, or are in nonstandard jobs such as contracts or part-time, retire later than those in a traditional job. Two thirds of older workers (defined as 55-64) who work part-time do so by choice. They tend to prefer a change of pace to retiring. The survey also found that university educated individuals are more likely than those without a degree to return to work after retiring, or to keep working.[11]

- *Legal changes* included legislation amending the Human Rights Code in Ontario that saw elimination of mandatory retirement effective as of December 2006. Mandatory retirement is still permitted to a varying degree in several provinces. Elimination of mandatory retirement gives mature workers more flexibility but there are significant regulatory barriers to the implementation of flexible retirement arrangements and uncertainty around availability of group benefits for employees 65+.[12]

- *Potential care-giving responsibilities* Women traditionally worked in non-paying homemaking and parenting roles where one is on call continuously with no direct pay and little recognition. The generation of women currently turning 60 has drawn attention to this inequity, and one wonders how they will negotiate the care-giving activities within their families, and what creative new solutions may emerge.
Gabliani found in her study that younger women may be more likely to keep working if a husband

becomes ill.[13] Retirement decisions would impact aged parents as well as ailing spouses, who may need on-going care from some source. As the trend is to push health care into the home and expect community and family to take on the responsibility, this will become an issue. It's not clear whether women will assume this role as they carry on their careers, or look for other solutions. In relationships where couples shared responsibilities this is yet another life stage to negotiate. It is new territory since fewer women in earlier generations worked outside the home; they therefore were more available when needed for caretaking. The presence of a spouse, dependent child or sibling who will require assistance due to health concerns is a reality for many to incorporate in their planning.

- In *dual career families* decisions will be made about how, whether or when each partner changes their career course and how the years and energy beyond mid-life will be invested. As options increase in the amount of time available to spend in leisure versus employment or volunteering, or combinations of the above, there will be many decisions to be negotiated.

  In my study the professional women said they were reluctant to retire in the traditional way. They value their professional role as it provides a source of financial independence, confidence and respect within society. They strove within their educational settings, families, and workplaces to attain this role. As Judith Finlayson found in her Canadian study of women's involvement in the work place, they have felt that they were swimming upstream "against the current"; they have survived through perseverance and determination.[14]

- *Gender differences* In a recent study of gender differences and marital quality of couples' work-to-retirement transitions, 700 soon-to-retire, newly retired and retired men and women, Moen found that men were more influenced by the financial incentives (62% as opposed to 40% for women) and women were more influenced than men in the timing of their retirement by the spouse's retirement (33% women and 9% men).[15] In my study women mentioned that connections, friends and community would continue to be important in their lives. A specific example of attachment to a community was a lesbian woman for whom having access to the gay community was an important advantage of maintaining ties with the city. The value of friendships will impact their decisions on where to live, or how to keep in touch with those who are important in their lives. People who have abandoned or modified the time spent in friendships during their most intense working periods may see retirement as a time to intensify these connections. We don't know yet.

As pioneers with no role models for how to combine family life and a career, they are still creating new realities by re-conceptualizing what this stage will be for them. A study showed that those who were highly satisfied with their jobs were less likely to view traditional retirement as a positive event.[16] Women who identified strongly with and had high commitment to their work have been found to view retirement negatively, as a threat to their self-concept.[17]

- "What are the attitudes, aspirations and concerns for mid-life professional women as they envisage retirement?" was the question of my doctoral research study. I subsequently interviewed men too and in the process asked if they considered themselves to be pioneers. Even though most of them expect that their retirements will be very different from that of their fathers, they didn't identify with that word. My hunch is that although men experienced changes throughout their adulthood, they didn't experience the same need for courage, creativity, intentionality and neither did they meet the resistance that the women encountered. Women were aware of taking a new, unbroken path, often having to push for what they wanted and proving themselves along the way. True pioneers.

- *Relationships* The patterns of our connections with family, friends and partners are changing. For committed couples currently in mid-life, the decisions and negotiations of what each person wants their retirement to be will again carve new patterns, as our generation has done throughout our adult lives.
  You can be married yet lonely within your relationship. Having experienced both a long-term marriage

and dating in mid-life, I find our generation is open to creating life patterns and living arrangements that honor themselves and their well-being. Committed and married couples, especially those in second relationships, are not always living together permanently but traveling to see their own grown children or away on business. I expect that these patterns will continue to become more diverse and accepted as realities become more complex.

You may have remained single in your life and have friends, lovers and family with whom you are emotionally intimate. Oral contraception, which came to market in the 1960s, made sex freer of consequences as we came of age. Through the course of the boomers' lives, changing norms and laws have continued to broaden our relationship options. We're a generation who tended to condone pre-marital sexual activities of our own children in ways that our parent's generation did not. In my experience, and as shown in the recent study *Sex and the seasoned woman: Pursuing the passionate life* by Gail Sheehy, this generation as it ages is exploring numerous ways to share both physical and emotional intimacy and sustain relationships of significance in our lives.[18]

- *Technology* is changing the way that people connect, learn and do research. People I know are part of communities that meet regularly on-line, sometimes with a purpose, and sometimes just to stay in touch. Professional associations offer learning events and forums on-line and via telephone conferencing.

Through internet we can keep connected with family and friends when we travel. Technology allows people to work from a second home or while traveling. I have friends who have kept serving their coaching clients while sailing on their boats in another hemisphere or while staying at a cottage. Who knows what the future may bring.

- *Working longer related to increase in self employment and other work arrangements.* Working provides psychological, social and economic benefits and allows the opportunity to compare yourself to others and to test your personal limits in productive activity, resulting in a sense of personal mastery. Women in my study were reluctant to retire especially if they have unfinished work agendas, perhaps due to starting their professional careers late. They had little interest in early retirement or in coinciding their retirement with their spouse's retirement; they had more desire to work past the traditional retirement age. They expected they would gradually decrease the amount that they work and would work at things that interested them for as long as they had the energy and interest. Women have long defined work as broader than being paid for meaningful tasks.

- *The Cornell Well-being and Retirement Study* found that there's a fundamental shift in how baby boomers view retirement, compared to their parents' generation. Boomers intend to remain active, work longer, travel more, volunteer their time and even return to school. For them retirement seems to be more a lifestyle transition than an end in itself.[19]

- Dr. Richard Haid has coined the term "Third Quarter of Life" suggesting that although there are no specific age markers in general at this stage of our lives the following occurs:
  - life becomes more important than work
  - it is not necessarily the end of work, but work becomes more on your terms
  - harvesting and using more of your wisdom
  - developing a life that you may have always hoped for but that is now possible![20]

- Although there will be some WOOPIES (well off older people), Simon-Rusinbowitz suggests that the majority of boomers will not be financially secure at age 67.[21] Fewer people have access to a company pension due to adjustments in the workplace and resultant shorter tenure, the technology bubble burst and the impact of the sub-prime mortgage and global economic crisis of late 2008. Many people have seen their retirement financial plans dramatically change.

- Merril Lynch and Ken Dychtwald produced The ML New Retirement Survey in 2005, which alerted the financial service industry that current planning models fail to capture the complexity of the boomer's retirement plans and aspirations. The study, based on a survey of the general population confirmed that boomers are not interested in pursuing a traditional model of leisure and the majority (76%) plans to work in some capacity. Forty-two percent want to cycle between periods of work and leisure, 16% want to work part-time, 13% want to start their own business and only 6% plan to work full-time. Two-thirds said it isn't about earning money but rather having mental stimulation.[22]

- Regarding travel, there's a change from the move-to-Florida-play-golf-and-die generation. Many tend to look for something more adventurous and unusual. Eldertreks is one adventure company for the 50 plus market. Art Pierce, a professor of marketing at Ryerson University, in Toronto says that to successfully target boomers, marketers must look at lifestyle, family circumstances and psychographics rather than age alone.[23]

How will you live the next chapter of your life? A large number of us are in the process of making and re-making those decisions. I'll share ideas that people are trying and through your choices you will show us what matters to you, and what you will do in mid-life and beyond. Let's get started to design your future.

Part Two

Creating Your Options

Chapter 4

Reviewing and Dreaming

Looking backwards and forwards

*Mid-life is a perfect time to stand wherever you are,
look with curiosity into your past,
honour who you genuinely are,
and open courageously to the future,
and to what you'd like to create.*

In chapter two you assessed the components of well-being that are relevant for you. In this chapter we'll pick up the process by looking backwards, and then forwards in your life. Mid-life is an ideal time to do so as it can be a rich time of insight, realignment and confirmation. As we become aware that life is finite we benefit from reflecting on where we are in our lives. Regrets may surface. We may judge or celebrate previous decisions. Hopefully, we acknowledge what is and isn't working. It's a time to clarify what you'd like your future to look like. Ideally, you'll see mid-life as the normal life transition that it is.

Jean Shinoda Bolen, a professor and Jungian analyst, wrote the story of her own mid-life pilgrimage at age 50 in *Crossing to Avalon*. She noted that mid-life is about reflection on the choices that you've made and potentially a time of spiritual awakening. Although the journey is an inward one, she believes that the telling of one's life story is an important part of the process, as it contributes to personal meaning making.[1]

Reviewing – reconsider your history

If we know how to work with it, the topography of our life journey holds a wealth of information or clues to help us to understand ourselves better and to make good decisions for our futures. In this chapter you can do activities that I use with my clients, and discover your profile.

STEP TWO looks at your strengths, personality, interests, values, and specific circumstances in your life that need to be accommodated. It's important to know what you bring to the table and where you get stuck. Be brave here. I've done these activities myself and they can provide rich insights. By the end of this section you'll be aware of the patterns or themes of how your life flows. Authenticity is the password, so take a deep breath and be honest. There are no wrong answers.

Activities

Activity #1

Take a blank piece of paper, turn it sideways, and draw a straight line, horizontally, across the middle of the page.

The far left side of the paper represents your birth, and the far right side represents your current age.

Indicate both the important high (above the line) and low (below the line) points of your life so far, from your perspective, in relationship to the neutral line. You may have had a seemingly incidental event that you experienced as a high point – go with that. This is totally subjective. Losing a job could have been a high point for you, and a low point to someone else. The goal is not to analyze our life in minute detail, but to capture what you perceive, in hindsight, to be the major peaks and valleys. You may even want to join the dots to visually capture the ride.

What observations do you make as look at your lifeline?

Are there surprises for you? If so, in what way?

Is there a theme underlying why you chose the events you did, or what makes them seem positive or negative to you? If so, what information does that provide for you about what is important to you? For example, was there a theme linking your relationships, or your achievements or times of freedom or lack of freedom in your life, or learning or adventure? The possibilities are endless. What popped into view for you?

Does the pattern of what emerged for you focus on a specific stage or aspect of your life?

Is there anything about the "highs" that tell you what to keep including in your life? Do the "lows" suggest what to address in your personal growth, or to stay away from as you plan your next step?

Activity #2

The following activity may strike you as daunting. It's preferable for you to answer all the questions; but remember you're in charge, so you may prefer to select just the ones that are helpful to you. Do what works for you. These are the most powerful questions I ask my clients to get at who they are. Everyone is unique. You want to build your future on who you are, so you set yourself up for success.

Start as far back as you can recall. If you can't remember something or you don't want to explore it then move on. This is not therapy but just a way to capture what really matters in your life. You may want to record your answers in writing, or by audio recording. You may prefer to have someone you trust ask you the questions, although you may benefit from having reflection time for your responses. It makes a wonderful legacy piece. I have a recording of my father's career history discussion we had in his sixties – a process he appreciated sharing at the time, and that I treasure years later.

Elementary school and your childhood

What did you like most about this stage?

What did you like least?

What were your most and least favorite subjects?

What subjects did you do best in?

Describe your involvement in hobbies, clubs or other activities.

Were you involved in sports, and if so, how was that for you? Did you prefer individual or team activities?

If you moved from one school or community to a new one, how did that go for you – was it difficult, or not, and in what way?

What did you dream of becoming "when you grew up"?

What did your parents want you to become?

What title would you use to describe that chapter of your life?

High school and your teen years

What do you remember most about this stage?

How was your transition to high school?

If you moved from one school or community to a new one, how did that go for you – was it difficult, or not, and in what way?

What did you like most, and least about high school?

What were your most and least favorite subjects?

What subjects did you do best in?

Describe your involvement and experience in any clubs, sports, extra-curricular activities and dating?

What roles did you play in activities – for example leadership, support, organizer, and how was that for you?

Did you have a favorite teacher and if so, what did you like about him or her?

Did you have part-time or summer employment, and if so, doing what? What did you like most and least about it?

What was your experience with authority figures?

What did you dream of becoming "when you grew up"?

What did your parents want you to become?

What were the best, and worst, aspects of your teen years?

What title would you use to describe that chapter of your life?

In your 20s and beyond (for each program of additional education or credentialing)

What education did you consider and choose after high school and why?

What process did you use to make that choice?

Where did you think it would lead for you?

Did you move out or live at home and how was that?

How easy or difficult was the adjustment to post-secondary education?

What did you like most and least about your program?

What were your most and least favorite subjects?

What subjects did you do best in?

Describe your involvement and experience in any clubs, sports, extra-curricular activities, and dating?

What roles did you play in your activities – such as leadership, support, organizer and how was that for you?

What role did relationships with your peers play in your life?

Did you have part-time or summer employment and if so, doing what? What did you like most and least about it?

What was your experience with authority figures?

What did you dream of becoming "when you grew up"?

What did your parents want you to become?

What title would you use to describe that stage or chapter of your life?

In your 20s and beyond (work and career).[2]

I suggest you reflect on these questions for each significant work role that you've had. If you invested time in a sabbatical, childrearing, or had a period of unemployment, use that as a stage too. Include contracts, volunteer roles or anything that is relevant for you.

List the jobs you've had since high school.

How did you get each job?

Which jobs did you enjoy most and why?

Consider any significant training, retraining, or sabbaticals that you had and describe how that came to be.

What skills did you like using?

What skills have you been told that you're good at?

Choose a few words or phrases to describe your personality.

Which aspects of your career do or did you dislike and why?

What disappointments did you encounter along the way and how did you deal with them?

Why did you take certain positions or moves?

Did you initiate changes or were they offered to you?

Why did you change from one thing to another and how did you make the changes?

Were there times you held back from taking a position or trying for something new? If so, why?

On a scale of 1-10, with 10 being the most, how much did your career(s) suit you?

Of what are you most proud? What were your major accomplishments?

What was missing for you?

What was your experience with authority figures?

If you had it to do again, what would you do differently?

What advice would you give to someone starting a career?

What title would you use to describe that chapter of your life? You may want to do it by decades – 20s, 30s, 40s or any categories that make sense from your life.

Personality and lifestyle

Do you prefer to keep busy or have time to make sense of your inner thoughts, feelings or desires?

Do you problem-solve in your head and need private time to do so, or do you prefer talking about your problem out loud?

Do you like group activities or prefer working independently?

Do you like taking a formal or informal leadership role or neither?

Do you like to connect socially with people in-depth or minimally?

Are you comfortable being on your own, or does that make you lonely or anxious?

Do you enjoy activities that provide the opportunity for you to discover or contribute the depth of your insights?

Is it important for you to be exposed to new things and ideas?

Do you approach new things cautiously, and prefer the known to the novel?

Are you better at seeing the big picture or at being detail-oriented?

Are you impulsive or cautious?

Do you get bored easily?

Are you most comfortable when doing things the way you have done them in the past?

Is it important for you to have the freedom to change course or your decision as new information becomes known?

Are you more comfortable finding new ways to do things or doing things the way you know how?

Do you prefer to work fairly constantly or with bursts of energy?

How would you characterize your personal relationships?

In the various chapters of your life, how have you apportioned time between your work or school and your personal life?

Outside of work do you spend more time alone, with colleagues, friends or family?

Are you in a committed relationship and if so, what is the quality of that relationship?

How much time do you currently share with that person?

Do you have hobbies and if so, which do you enjoy most and why?

In what ways do you manage stress in your life? How successful are you in managing stress?

What was the best vacation that you've ever had and what made this so for you?

What was the best year of your life so far and what makes this so?

Considering all the places you've lived in your life, which place did you like best and why? Do you like where you currently live and why or why not?

Do you have a solid understanding of your financial circumstances? Note the limitations and opportunities it presents for you.

What are you most proud of as you reflect on your personal life to date?

Discover your patterns

Looking back at your responses –

What themes do you see in your choices?

What roles do you like best?

How much people contact do you like or do you prefer to work independently?

Do you like meaningful interaction or small talk?

Do you maintain personal relationships over time?

When it comes to making your life be what you want it to be, what skills do you bring?

When you have overcome a real or perceived barrier and managed to pull things together in the end – What did you do to make that happen?

What did you learn about your decision making? Are you satisfied with the quality of your decisions or is there anything you'd like to do differently going forward?

What can you learn about your values in the decisions that you made regarding where to work, promotions and other choices? On what did you base your decisions?

How do you navigate times of change or transition? Are they easy or difficult for you? What is your style to manage change?

Do you set unrealistic goals so that you avoid true success or failure?

When you run into challenges, how do you deal with them? How do you get going again?

Do you prefer to plan things in advance?

Are you most comfortable with a predictable rhythm to your life?

Are you uncomfortable if you have unscheduled time?

When do you feel most alive? What are you doing, where are you, with whom? Perhaps close your eyes to get in touch with it. Be as detailed as you can be.

What has motivated you in your career and personal life? Do you have a sense that there's a purpose to your life and if so, what is that?

If you're considering leaving work life as you currently know it, what do you anticipate that you will miss most?

What have you always wanted to do but been afraid to do?

Do you have any regrets and if so, what are they?

What are you telling yourself that isn't true of you any more?

When you were going through this review process, was there any specific time in your life that you got excited or nostalgic about as you thought of it? If so what was it about it that touched you? This is indicative of something for which you have passion.

Is there anything about your current circumstances such as, for example, health conditions, financial realities or family responsibilities that you need to factor into your decisions?

If you're retired, what are you missing most? What surprises you?

What do you wish that people close to you really knew about you, but don't?

What else do you know about yourself that you need to consider in your next steps?

Reflect on what you've learned about yourself through this review. You may want to write a one-page summary of your "story" or a series of descriptors. In some way, capture what you're all about as you need to honor that as we move forward.

Dreaming – envisage your ideal future

At the end of our life we're often more disappointed by the things we didn't do than by the things we tried. So set aside your fears and for this step in particular, explore, dream and discover what you really long for.

Becoming clear about what matters most to us can provide the impetus to move us in the direction of designing our futures. Does that strike you as onerous, or exciting? It's important to get in touch with what ideal looks like to you – your version of heaven. I promise, we'll deal with practicalities later but pretend, for now, that anything is possible.

I chose the word "dream", because I want you to open to the most desirable possibilities for yourself. Almost too good to be true! If the word "dream" doesn't work for you, substitute "aspiration," or "goal" or whatever allows you to imagine a future worth stretching for. Do you hear yourself saying any of these to yourself right now?

- I need to have the possibility more formed in order to accept it or I prefer to know how plausible the idea is or what I'd need to do or how much money I'd need to make it come true.

- I don't want to set myself up for disappointment by getting an ideal situation in mind and then discovering down the road that it isn't attainable.
- I think dreaming and imagination aren't as valuable as rational thought with facts and figures.
- I'm just not that good at it.
- I feel overwhelmed by letting anything seem possible.

In STEP THREE you'll benefit by dreaming as large as you can. I'll share specific activities that you can do. Here are some guidelines:
Think of your whole life
Dream as if anything is possible
Dream your own dream
Dream forward, from who you are today
Get help if you need it
Treat this as the important activity that it is

Think of your whole life

Consider yourself from the broadest perspective possible. People often focus on what activities might replace their present job or career, but we can get pleasure and a sense of accomplishment from many sources. If you're focused narrowly on your career persona, this may be more difficult. Remember the many components of well-being from chapter two. Cast your gaze broadly at this juncture to consider more than just your career self.

In career transition consulting when clients lost their jobs, they'd often say in hindsight that they'd been given the gift of a chance to re-examine what they really wanted. A health scare can offer the same opportunity. And so can retirement. There are 24 hours to each day for the rest of your life; how do you want to spend that resource?

Dream as if anything is possible

Get even the fragment of an idea down. Brainstorm without judging, at this point, how realistic it seems. You may dream of owning a sail boat and sailing six months of the year. The end result may be that you are co-owner of a boat and crew in a vacation destination for two weeks a year, but at least you headed in that direction.

One friend who is a sailor announced a few years ago that she had long dreamed of doing some serious sailing in the Mediterranean. Just recently she did some traveling in Europe where she crewed aboard a 40-foot yacht in the Cyclades and then helped to deliver the boat to Crete. On the same adventure, she found herself racing in a regatta in the north of Ireland and exploring the Oslo fjord. Had she not acknowledged her dream, then that would never have happened.

By mid-life we may have imposed limitations on what we believe is possible for us. These may be legends that evolved from what someone told us when we were young or how we've lived life so far. In my experience we're capable of much more than we think we are. *Don't put limits on your dream.*

Dream your own dream

If your dream looks the same as your parent's life, then make sure it's really your dream, not one that you inherited due to your lack of creativity or courage. If you're in a relationship I suggest that you each explore your dream as individuals first. If one of you is so wedded to a specific dream being fulfilled that there is no room for the other partner's dream to be respected, then you may want to look to how your decisions have been made as a couple. Look at the pattern of your relationship and each of your personality preferences. Exploring how you can work to co-create a future that works for both of you as a couple will increase your chances of success in transitioning this stage. It requires honesty and excellent communication skills. This is a circumstance when assistance in the form of a counselor or coach may be beneficial if these skills aren't strengths of your relationship.

Dream forward, from who you are today

Don't hold onto a dream you had at 21 if it's outdated. You update your wardrobe, sports equipment and technology, so why not your dreams? Be sure you're dreaming forward.

Some people set a goal out of school, get on a treadmill and never reflect on whether what they want has changed. They may complain to those around them, but aren't able or willing to find a way to change their circumstances. Many people let life happen *to* them.

Get help if you need it

You're the best expert on yourself and may know what you're passionate about and value most. If you don't have that awareness after working through this whole process, then consider seeking help one-on-one from someone like a life coach or another professional who can facilitate your finding clarity. It's common in mid-life to invest in intentional reflection and make that a priority.

If you're an impulsive, action-oriented personality type, this may take some discipline and feel uncomfortable. It can take a long time, yet makes a huge difference in your happiness and for those around you. False starts take time too, so do it with intention the first time.

Treat this as the important activity that it is

Get in the right mood. If this isn't the right time for you to really get into this, then figure out a time that is and plan for it. Consider going somewhere or doing an activity that takes you out of your ordinary life and environment. Surround yourself with whatever brings you pleasure and makes you and life seem special. Don't judge what emerges at this point. Just capture what comes to mind. Record your ideas. Even little things can be important. Grasping a thread of your dream can be the first step to allow you to weave it over time into a whole. It doesn't have to arrive full blown.

I had occasion to renew and reinvent my life at mid-life and learned that I benefited by giving the process space and time. I found it difficult to accept the truth of the degree of unhappiness in my personal life but, as at age 18, my body was what finally captured my attention. The cause and symptoms were different but it was clear to me that I needed to listen. Through that journey I used many of the tools I'm suggesting to you and fed myself through body, mind and spiritual portals.

My journey was a considered detour from the path I was on. Yet the rewards of being authentic have been great. Through the process I re-owned who I am and experienced true intimacy, growth and relationships with wonderful people along the way. It wasn't all smooth sailing. I learned as much from the challenges as I did the successes. I'd wanted to write this book in 2000 but it's a better book now because I'm able to integrate what I've learned from going through my own transition along with sharing my research findings.

Take the time to check in with and create your version of your dream for the future or it may not happen. A future will happen, but it may not fit you. The key is to start the process early, make it a priority and expect surprises. It is through trusting yourself to open to possibilities and not judge the process that the magic can occur.

Hints and suggestions

- Do the activities when you feel confident and optimistic.
- Ideas may come to you while standing in the shower following playing an intense sports game where your mind has cleared while focusing on the sport, or while walking in the rain.

- Get a journal and keep it handy for you to record in when ideas come to you.
- If you get an idea, record it on anything handy so that you remember it. Napkins in coffee shops are common tools!
- Exchange homes with a friend for a designated time. You'll be out of your routine and not tempted to be distracted by chores. Then you can dream.
- Take time on your commute to reflect.
- If you prefer structure, engage in a program, book, workshop or event designed to lead you through a process.
- Go to a retreat or spa with the intent to listen to your inner self. Befriend the silence, use candles, luxuriate in a bath, set aside your emails and phone calls, eat alone, and order room service. Do whatever it takes to break out of your routine and hectic pace.
- Go into nature or to a favorite place in the country or near the water to find some time to be alone with your inner thoughts.
- If you're on a plane trip, use the time to record your thoughts while you're literally "in the clouds." Believe that anything possible.
- Listen to classical or ambient music, if that opens you to hear your feelings and to imagine possibilities.

- Go to an all-inclusive resort where you can wander and be involved in your reflections. It's especially great if there's a beach with an expansive horizon. Some people sail to an isolated spot to reflect.
- If you don't already know this skill, learn to quiet your mind, meditate or in some way listen to your intuition.
- Be creative by writing a poem, playing music, or capturing keywords about your future. Make a collage of pictures to capture a visual representation of your desired future, and post it to keep yourself motivated.
- Park your fear or skepticism and work through the activities. I've used all of them myself or with clients. Use what works for you and record your discoveries. Close your eyes and really explore the scene that emerges for you. Don't rush it. My experience with clients shows that deep inside you already have at least the beginnings of the answers to what your own ideal next chapter is all about. Take the time to get in touch with that part of yourself. Trust me this is a very important part of the process. Your future awaits.

Activities

Unfinished business

As you looked back at your review activities you may have found things that you had wished to do but never did. Perhaps you or someone in your family got sick, or a company was sold, or you divorced, or you relocated with a spouse, or had a maternity leave, or you didn't have the qualifications. This is an opportunity to focus honestly on any regrets that you have. Take your time and consider these questions before we proceed:

Record dreams from your past that you want, or need, to let go of.

Record dreams that you need to reclaim and consider working them into your future, even if they take a different shape at this point in your life.

What were you going to have accomplished by this age?

What "isn't written" that you're still wanting to do or experience?

Think of your next chapter – *think ideal*

What "must haves" and "must not haves" would be in your life?

What changes would you make to your life if you had unlimited resources?

What activities, people and things would you let go of?

What would keep you healthy?

What would you look forward to when you got up every day?

What would you do for fun?

What would you do for adventure, for new experiences and growth?

Where would you like to live? Describe it. Remember, it can be anything you want it to be at this point. Look around and imagine it in detail.

Would you have additional residences and if so, why, and where would they be?

Would you want to travel, or not? If so, to where and how often? Describe it as fully as you can.

What would give your life meaning? What does your heart yearn to do?

To whom or for what cause, would it matter that you're still alive?

It can take a while to get at what's underneath the stories of our life, yet it's a critical part of good mid-life career or retirement planning. Especially if your life review has shown you to have a pattern of denial or jumping into new ventures too quickly, slow down and decide to invest in scoping this next important life stage more intentionally. Getting out of your normal pace may be uncomfortable for action-oriented or impulsive individuals but it's an important key to unlock the door of our true dreams.

I wrote the following poem during my own mid-life process a few years ago. As I became clear about my regrets and parts of myself I needed to reclaim I was left with the responsibility of filling the new canvas, unclear how much and who in my current life would be able to go forward with me.

The Mid-life Journey

The necessary pull to look back, review and reclaim my place – the meaning of my life

Me as an individual, without the roles that society expects

What is the authentic piece?

Who is the real me if I am not the roles?

What is my uniqueness?

What feeds my passion?

Children have provided the flowering of lost parts of self like a greenhouse reflecting light to the outer world while inside is a warm gestation of spirit

Mid-life empowers me to refocus, embrace the chance to integrate my learning and self-discovery from all of life's experiences

Enough of life lived to see patterns and discard false starts and choose to respect, nurture and rediscover the inner truth...a liberation

Concurrently a fearful and exciting time of getting rid of hollow and outlived parts

Tending to the early child so long ago quieted – to give a paintbrush to the new me, to pull from the colours, smells and sensations of my imagination

And move towards creatively expressing and contributing to the universe the uniqueness of my soul

Urgency

Choose an age to which you expect to live and calculate the number of years you have left.

If you had one month to live, ask yourself what you would do, in as much detail as possible, with that time.

What is the one thing that if you don't do before you die, you will feel unfulfilled?

What is holding you back from doing that?

Do you have a cause to which you need to contribute something as part of your legacy?

Listen to the words of Tim McGraw's 2004 song that invites us to "Live like you were dying."[3]

Flow

Csikszentmihalyi's far-reaching study of thousands of individuals looks at how we live fully in carrying out our everyday lives while still experiencing connection to the universe. He introduced the term "flow" to describe that state.[4]

When do you feel the most at ease in your life?

When do you lose track of time? What are you doing, where are you, with whom? What do you see, hear, and feel?

What have you done, or what would you do, without compensation, that has brought you satisfaction? Be specific about the source of your satisfaction.

To be passionate about something means to be connected inwardly to our own spirit and uniqueness. How will this show up in your next life chapter?

Chapters

What do you know now that you didn't know a decade ago?

Pretending that each chapter of your life has a title, what chapter title are you leaving?

How many more chapters are there to your life?

What is that next chapter for?

What would you like to call your next chapter?

Epitath

Imagine that you've lived a full life and that you've died peacefully of natural causes. A memorial service is being held and you can visualize who is there and what is happening at the service. If you're comfortable, really go there.

How are you being remembered by the people that matter most to you?

What is it about you and your life that they're referring to that touches you most?

Do you have any regrets or things you wished you had done or said?

Ethical will

An ethical will is a document that we write to loved ones in our lives to record and bequeath to them the wisdom, values and life lessons that our life has gifted to us.

Andrew Weil has researched the history of this tool and believes that it has great contemporary relevance. He invites us to consider writing an ethical will to help us to make sense of our lives and the fact of our aging. He includes a portion of his own in his book.[5]

Write your ethical will including such things as setting out your beliefs about life, the wisdom that you've gained through living so far and what you know to be true.

Summary

Reflect on your insights and record what you learned about what would make your next life chapter perfect for you. What is your dream? Be as specific as you can.

Chapter 5

Creating Potential Options

Customizing your future

*Life is not a linear journey.
It is more like a spiral circling around,
renewing and reinventing itself as it goes.
We are designed for possibility.*

Pulling it together

How are you doing? You may feel overwhelmed. I expect there's lots of information and loose ends floating around. I hope that you're tracking what you're discovering about yourself as we go along. It may feel messy right now, but these are important elements that when combined create your options.

Let's proceed to STEP FOUR by integrating your insights from the *components of well-being, reviewing, and dreaming activities,* seeing how they fit together and beginning to formulate ideas to explore. This lets you prioritize what matters most to you so you can see possibilities emerge. I suggest that you decide on a time frame for the next life chapter that you're considering and develop two or three potential options. Are you in mid-career and wanting to set a goal for 10 years down the road? Perhaps you're planning to leave full-time work in 2 years and want to find a new meaning to your life or are retired and wanting to find new challenges.

> *What priorities did you identify for yourself related to establishing and maintaining components of well-being in chapter two?*
> *What ideas do you have on how to incorporate them?*

> *What did you learn from the reviewing activities in chapter four?*
> *List what specifically you need to get more information on.*

> *What did you learn about your ideal future from the dreaming activities in chapter four?*
> *What do you know and how well developed are your dream ideas at this point?*

You may be clear on your next steps. You may just want to *rebalance* your current life. Perhaps you want to *renew* an old interest, add a new element to your life, or desire a serious overhaul – what participants in my research called a *reinvention.*

When you look at your summary information what is clear? It may be just the start of an idea or something may be very obvious to you. For example, you may know that your priority will revolve around moving to a warmer climate. Or perhaps you know that you want or need to continue earning money, or do aspects of what you did in a job that you enjoyed years ago. You may have an over-riding issue such as being close to elderly parents until they no longer need your care.

Keep these issues in mind as I present what research shows mid-life people consider in their decisions. I'll also present some examples of people's situations to give you ideas. Then you'll start to create your own. You may be impatient to get to a clear answer for yourself. People who are most successful stay positive during the uncertainty of the quest and keep open during the research and reality checking phases to the options ripening as the process proceeds.

Start by looking at your situation at a high level to see if it fits into one of these categories. Decide if you're leaning towards *rebalancing, renewing, or reinventing* your current life. There is often overlap among these.

Rebalancing

Rebalancing means changing how you apportion the components in the well-being section and how they align with other aspects of your life and priorities. It may mean creating options to allocate your time differently, or investing in new skills to expand an undeveloped part of yourself. For some it will focus on a pivotal area needing more attention. Here are some examples:

Don, at age 57 realized through his review that he wanted to do more physically in order to stay healthy going forward. He'd danced professionally early in his life. Although he couldn't do that any more, he reframed what was possible and developed a plan to include something he loved that kept him in shape and let him enjoy time with friends who enjoyed dancing. He decided to rent a studio to dance free form a few times a month and shared that opportunity with his friends. He made it into a community of sorts. It was a fun, creative activity that he was also able to offer to women he dated.

Tina, in her late 40s was a senior manager at a pharmaceutical company. She loved what she did, yet had been feeling burnt out the last several years. She traveled and commuted a lot for work and had a young second family that she didn't see as often as she wished. When she looked at her situation from a broader perspective she realized that, despite having excellent childcare, she had let go of some of her parenting intentions. Tina came to an agreement with her employer to work from home three days a week when she wasn't out of town. She finds she's able to get more done without the commute plus she's there when her children get home from school. They've learned to respect her closed door and not disturb her when she's working. Now she has better work-life balance. This arrangement has led her to start thinking of researching a related entrepreneurial venture for her future to give her more flexibility.

Does anything need to be rebalanced in your life?

Renewing

Renewing often involves picking up an earlier, unlived part of yourself that you've rediscovered and are now reclaiming. You may want to focus on what needs your attention or what's not working in your life. Then work to nurture that part and build options around it. Sometimes at mid-life it's ourselves that we've lost. It may be that there is an unlived dream that ignites your passion in life and will pull you towards it. Sometimes it's wanting to keep working but needing a new environment or focus.

Ron, in his mid-40s, had felt unfulfilled as a partner in a large professional firm. He wanted more balance in his life and to feel that what he was doing mattered to him. When his review highlighted his strong philanthropic values, he researched options, left the partnership and went to a CFO role in a not-for-profit organization. That opened him up to do networking and establish his credibility in that sector. He sees himself staying involved in this, in some capacity, for as long as he's able to contribute. He and his wife share an interest in adventure traveling and are exploring ways to combine that and his skills in finance in a volunteer capacity in international placements over the upcoming decades.

Scott completed a graduate degree in mid-life during which aspirations surfaced that had been submerged in the earlier years of marriage and raising a family. It also reinvigorated dreams of having a wider experience. He arranged with his employer for a transfer for three years from Canada to New Zealand. The relocation required some risk as there was no guarantee of re-employment upon his return to Canada. His son remained in university in Canada and his daughters and wife set out with him on the adventure. Catharine, who had been primarily a stay at home mom, enrolled in university which set her on a new path as well. Upon their return to Canada, Scott and Catharine both commenced new jobs. The outcome of the whole experience was one of tremendous personal and professional growth, individually and as a couple. If you're creative, renewal can be a win-win and expansive experience.

Is renewal a part of your future?

Reinventing

Reinventing is more than an "add on." It can mean changing how you're living by heading in a different direction or changing the structures of your life. It may involve finding a new occupation, a new role, different lifestyle or relocating.

Elizabeth has valued establishing and nurturing community spirit. It was at the core of her teen and adult activities. Her husband John is a creative and personable engineer. Elizabeth, a social worker in her early work life, had set up programs and established a community center in a rural setting where they lived. Their project for their 50s, as their children leave home, is to turn their home into a facility where they can host events while respecting the history of the venue. Although they're not certain how it will evolve, their valuing of community, connecting people and honoring heritage is at the core of their plans for the next stage of their lives.

Lauren, a successful university program director, wanted a break from cold, dark Canadian winters. She explored options, and in her 50s rented out her house, and with the agreement of her employer, did a three-year contract on a different continent. This increased her impact internationally in her professional area, offered her learning opportunities about a different culture and provided numerous adventures. Lauren is now well-positioned for when she leaves full-time employment to do more international work through her new contacts in other countries, and she has confidence in what's possible.

Andrejs Berzins has taken his life-long litigation experience and his criminal law and procedure expertise to various legal projects inside and outside Canada to build better legal systems for the democratic public, wherever they may be. He worked in Latvia on special assignments. His advice for lawyers afraid that retirement is to be feared or endured: "Be creative. Be ready to take a risk!"[1]

The following is an example of a man who apparently integrated aspects of rebalancing, renewing and reinventing himself.

Dr. Hugh Thomson former surgeon at the Hospital for Sick Children in Toronto retired and started woodcarving. His skill is so developed that he is now teaching at the Academy of Artisans. He also became an executive member of the Ontario Woodcarver's Association. "Thomson [now] considers himself an artist and teacher. The redirection of his surgical talents into carving in local woods such as basswood and butternut seems like him a natural transition."[2]

Trends

- exchanging houses (city, rural, cross country, international) informally with people you know or through an established house-exchange network
- singles sharing houses to free up money for travel or other adventures or setting up a home business
- people with second properties mutually sharing one of the properties in a city for business opportunities or to be close to family
- working half-year at a seasonal job and traveling the other half
- self-employed people finding work or consulting or volunteer opportunities in areas of the world where they want to travel and combining the two; couples coordinating their professional activities with their personal in a joint way to increase leisure
- contracting with your employer to take an extended sabbatical, or propose combining an interest you have with a special project that would add value to your employer and international partnering

- downsizing your living space or moving from owning to renting in order to free up money for priorities
- changing to a less responsible job or something new
- looking at the skills you like using and are good at, and considering whether there's another work environment to do it in, maybe instead of a large corporation considering a smaller organization focused on a cause that you believe in
- working with an independent financial planner to assess alternatives and tax implications of your options

Jonathan and Fern, a couple in their 60s, had an interesting opportunity come their way. Fern had mainly been a consultant and at mid-life Jonathan had taken early retirement from his employer to pursue a consulting career. When asked to bid on a contract in a developing country they jumped at it. They'd already started to think about moving from their house into a condominium. After seeking advice from their financial planner and accountant, they became clear on how they could benefit from this opportunity. They'd be able to do work they enjoyed, help the people of that country, have an adventure, and benefit financially. It required them to sell their current house, put their belongings into storage, sever all ties to Canada such as bank accounts and stay out of the country a specific percentage of each year. When they returned to Canada they would have three years worth of tax free income and have experienced doing work they loved.

Jeff wanted an enjoyable part-time job after leaving full-time employment. He loved golf, was good at it and had great interpersonal skills so we built options for him to explore based on those aspects. We brainstormed a list of possibilities. Through his review, we knew how far he wanted to commute from home, how frequently he wanted to work and what his other strengths were. Here are potential options for him to explore:

- working at a local golf club
- sales associate at a sports store selling equipment or golf clothes
- consulting on golf vacation holidays or packages for corporate events
- golf instructor for beginners, with a plan to retrain if he liked this and wanted to expand his involvement
- selling golf equipment to stores if you have sales skills
- marketing a new golf resort
- producing the newsletter for a private country club
- working part-time at something not golf related, and volunteering to coach for blind golfers

He chose a couple of options and began to gather information that will allow him to make the best decision about next steps.

Hints and suggestions

- *Watch what excites you* As you explore your options, notice what excites you most about ideas. Maintain that body-mind awareness we looked at in chapter two. Keep a "can do" attitude. Note those positive energy shifts in your body that indicate you're aligned with the idea. And note the times a suggestion feels "wrong" to you. Write the positive ones somewhere as clearly as you can, as they emerge.

- *Get help if you get stuck* Get assistance from others to help you generate ideas if you get stuck. Often we're too close to our own situations to see options. Share what you've learned about yourself so far with people you trust and see if they can give you suggestions of how your "must haves" can look when integrated.

- *Techniques* Give your next chapter a name or slogan that will motivate you. Choose a picture, song, or symbol to represent it.

- *Gather people you trust* and formalize a committee of advisors and make it a committed project. Imagine how you'll feel when it becomes truly realized. Ask yourself why your goal is worth striving for and record your reasons.

- *Keep communicating to those in your life* It can take significant time to prepare for a life change. Keep others involved in your process. Remember that you can't be responsible for someone else living unhealthily or out of balance. Try and involve them in creating positive changes in their life but you can only make changes for yourself. If you live with someone whose presence depletes you, consider the impact of that on your health going forward. Conversely, connection to people with whom you can share the spectrum of activities related to good health can contribute positively to your well-being. Communicate during your transition.

Considerations when creating options

In addition to my suggestion to keep communicating, the issues from my own and emerging research about what mid-life people consider as important when making future-oriented decisions include:

>   Having a meaningful purpose to life
>   Connection and relationship with others
>   Learning and growth
>   Where to live
>   Travel

What is your meaningful purpose in life?

During unplanned career transitions clients mentioned things from the following list as what they would miss about their job:

>   challenge
>   contributing
>   feeling part of something
>   friends
>   growth

identity
learning new things
money
nothing
people
power
recognition
routine
status

You've reflected on what matters most to you in your work and personal life in our previous activities. Try and put that understanding as it relates to your "purpose going forward" into one sentence.

Here are ways that their purpose played out in the following people's lives:

Bryan has been an entrepreneur in his professional field and when he becomes less involved in his company, he plans to participate on committees for policy issues he cares about. Sometimes in later life we have sufficient financial resources to allow us to do things we've dreamt of for years. We may have fewer responsibilities and be more able to make changes in our lifestyle. Maybe we're determined to make this chapter of our life what we need it to be for our legacy, and will get creative in making that come true. He's driven by the urgency of environmental issues in the world and is in a transition of selling his company and joining a group of angel investors to back research that may provide solutions to our environmental challenges.

Ruth, a mid-life medical doctor, is in the process of getting a law degree in preparation for her version of retirement. She plans to combine medicine, law, and her interest in abused women and children to focus on working with causes close to her heart. She told me: "In the end I have such a strident feeling that I want to stop these things. You either help them, or you get away from it; I can't ignore them so I work in this field."

Amy, 62 wanted to combine her experience and interest in camping which began in her youth, her skills in her profession as a teacher and her life experience as a lesbian to assist gay, lesbian, and bisexual youth in her retirement. She isn't sure how yet but her purpose is clear. She and her long-term partner had a dream to build a retirement home out of the city. They have come to realize that so much of what's important to them in their role of helping others takes place in the more urban centers where greater population density means that organizations and activities for gay youth are within their community. So after much reflection and discussion they have decided not to relocate from the city.

How will you meet your connection and relationship needs?

Chances are if not you then someone close to you has been impacted by the changes, breakdown and increased diversity in family roles and structures over the past decades. These changes impact how couples and families relate and stay connected. In addition to intact long-term relationships, there are blended families, some couples are divorcing late, people have second families and grown children are involved in extended education or returning home after their own marriages end. Issues surrounding these connections may be a consideration in our retirement decisions.

Making new connections throughout our lives is an important activity. While preparing to spend time on the west coast I was able to correspond beforehand via internet with people who had similar interests. A man I met who was planning to return to the city I was visiting was doing the same thing from his current home in Australia in advance of his return to Canada.

Friendships may form an important base for us and provide continuity in our lives. Considering how to stay in touch with long-term friends as well as make new ones and ways that we will meet our relationship needs are relevant aspects to work into our plan.

Couples in a relationship will have important decisions to make about how, when, and if their careers change course and how the years beyond mid-life will unfold. Variables related to connection are pivotal to consider. Ask yourself:

How much social interaction do I need?

How much depth do I need in my relationships?

Are there groups that I interact with now which will change based on other decisions I may make such as moving, leaving work or traveling more?

What type and amount of social interaction do I want with my spouse on a daily or weekly basis?

This is especially worth reflecting on if you have spent most of your working lives apart due to the nature of the work life choices made.

How will you continue to learn and grow?

There are formal and informal ways to learn. Often this activity easily combines with other aspects of your dream. Here are a few ideas:
- attend a holiday with a sports clinic focus to learn or improve new skills
- go to a retreat with healthy food, beautiful surroundings and curious, empowered people in order to make connections and learn about a new part of the world
- attend an art school or continuing education program to learn a new skill, networking for work opportunities or for the skills you can learn
- attend cooking classes, perhaps by combining it with travel as a friend did when she went to France
- expose yourself to a new language using a self-study program and then travel to where that language is spoken to experience immersion
- revisit a previous dream

Psychology major *Saul Goldstein* made the dean's list at age 93 when he earned his B.Sc. from the University of Toronto in just over three years. He did so with high distinction marks and might go for a master's degree. His thirst for knowledge comes partly from the fact that his studies were interrupted as he migrated country to country in Europe during WW2. "The more you learn, the more you realize there is yet more to learn," he said.[3]

In 2005 *Sarah Jane Growe* was 66, retired, a grandmother of five, and had just completed her ME degree. She had returned to the University of British Columbia to complete the degree that she had started in 1971. Smith College started a program for women ages 23-85, who had interrupted their education; and they are now make up 8% of the undergraduate population. In 2002 the oldest woman graduated at age 87.[4]

Where do you want to live?

If you're considering re-locating the following are some considerations:
- proximity to activities that you're interested in, be they cultural, intellectual, spiritual, or recreational
- if you'll continue working, ensure that work is available for you there and that you have the provincial or state credentials needed, or include getting certified in your plan
- if travel is part of your plan, ensure you have accessibility to travel hubs
- availability of transit for socializing, entertainment and medical appointments, especially as we age
- keeping connected to out of town family and friends by having space for them to visit
- a few couples I know, currently in good health, built new homes in their 50s and had safety

bars installed and light switches at wheelchair height with future health uncertainty of themselves or friends in mind

- David Foot, a Canadian economist and professor, predicts that living near medical support and hospitals will be an important variable in coming real estate values; he says that boomers are less likely to relocate to a community that lacks a top-notch hospital[5]
- parents are living longer, so accessibility in order to participate in their care, being close to family and friends or other support networks is a consideration
- investigate fractional property ownership or time share options, so not as much of your money is tied up but you have access to a second property
- weigh the decisions of size and location of your home plus buying versus renting from both the rational financial and emotional perspectives
- your ability and the cost to get health insurance in the locale where you will live
- for implications of your choices on your financial situation consult with advisors so that you understand tax and legal consequences for your future, especially if investing in a second or out of country property
- before relocating to your vacation home community research the activities, weather and realities of it in all seasons

- keep in mind if you consider relocating just to be with your adult children that they may move or be transferred and that you would still have options for yourself
- acknowledge what you are moving away from as well as what you are moving towards when you make relocation decisions and consider that in the context of your well-being criteria

Ann's career was as a mother and part-time nurse and Sanjay was a long time municipal government manager with a pension and health benefits. They took retirement in their late fifties. Family and traditional values have been important to them. They worked for security and having enough money to provide for their children. They've both dreamed of having a place in Florida as their parents had. Their option is clear. They will spend winters in the south and summers at their family cottage with an occasional trip every few years. Their aspirations are not complex. Participating in a leisure activity in a climate they both like is what's important to both of them.

Is traveling for me?

Travel is an activity that people often say they want to do when they have more time or retire. Participants in my research mentioned the following reasons for wanting to travel: to learn, for mental stimulation, openness to a larger perspective on the world and different cultures, to see architecture, beautiful vistas, physical geography and for adventure.

Are you interested in travel? You may prefer the familiarity of your home and where you're most comfortable. Or you may be interested to simply read about different places or watch travel shows on television or attend a lecture on different parts of the world. You may be unable to travel due to a health condition or not be a curious person and prefer to invest your life energy in a smaller sphere.

Some people travel to a familiar vacation spot year after year, as it provides the feeling of being comfortable and in control in your surroundings or perhaps offers a nostalgic, emotional connection with important memories. Several people in my study were interested in combining professional skills and interests with travel. One woman planned to volunteer her dentistry skills in developing countries. Here are some considerations regarding travel:

- organized tours may work best if you like to know the plan ahead, and not want to deal with details or when time is limited or language is an issue or if you prefer to be social and in a group
- planning a visit to somewhere like Machu Picchu or the Camino de Santiago can combine training for fitness and a spiritual experience
- a group hiking or biking holiday in a foreign country means you can go into training ahead of the trip, polish up your language skills, set goals, experience connecting to nature in a beautiful countryside – this may integrate several elements of what's important to you:

purpose, connection, learning, physical and spiritual quests

A few years ago I took a cruise that catered to diverse interests. We visited a mediaeval town, islands that were the inspiration for classic mythological literature, beauty in the form of art, architecture and glass factories in Venice. The light refraction of Santorini offered artists and photographers memorable views and hills to climb. Some loved seeing where the Olympics originated or where the Trojan Horse was said to have been employed. And others liked the food and dancing on the ship. What do you want to experience or learn more about? Bring intent to your plans. What are you curious about? What do you want to plan to do or see? Create options that are right for you.

Wendy is a professional who was employed for a few years in her career, but mainly had her own consulting practice. She loves what she does. Being challenged, contributing to her profession, having freedom and being socially active are important to her. She enjoys traveling, socializing, skiing and owning a house. She has a self-funded pension plan and would like to work for as long as she still enjoys it, or needs to, to fund her lifestyle. She sees herself gradually winding down and becoming more selective with the contracts she seeks. A leader in her field she's able to weave attending and speaking at international conferences into opportunities to see new cities and countries and expand her network.

Are there any additional aspects about your specific situation that need to be considered?

- a health issue
- age and age differences if in a relationship
- career aspirations of either of you if in a relationship
- family for whom you're responsible
- financial resources
- transferable skills
- workplace restrictions and opportunities

In this chapter you've pulled together the important aspects of yourself from the components of well-being, reviewing and dreaming activities and have been presented with aspects that research shows we should consider to create options especially in mid-life and beyond. The activities in the next chapter will make the options more concrete. First, consider the following:

Activity

If you're able at this point, record up to three potential options.

For each option, what do you still need to find out in order to make a good decision?

If you don't have potential options framed yet, what do you still need to find out more information about in order to develop some options?

Chapter 6

Researching, Reality Checking and Planning

Spiraling towards clarity

*We must let go of what we thought our life would be
in order to open to what is waiting for us.
If we seek with true receptivity and curiosity
we will be gifted with our best next step.*

Does the above quotation seem incongruent with the chapter title to you? Successful people are able to engage in researching, reality checking and planning of action steps while remaining open to integrating what they find and reconfiguring their plans realistically. Both rigor and flexibility are required.

At this point you have either a list of information to start exploring, or potential options. STEP FIVE is to gather missing information, check your assumptions and plan your action steps. It's a process of spiraling between clarity and confusion as you do those activities. As you'll see in the next chapter attentive and honest exploration is often a way to test your desired direction. It can be a project that takes a substantial investment of time woven through your current life. If you're action oriented be careful to not be too impulsive. If you're reflective ensure you keep making contacts with people and gathering realistic information in the world. The good news is that your decisions will be more sound and your transition easier if you engage patiently and enthusiastically in this step.

The things you need to research may include such activities as: exploring work opportunities, places to travel to, your financial situation, organizations to volunteer with, boards to be on or communities to live in or visit. Gathering information might open new possibilities that are even more exciting than your current vision of your future. You may have extensive lists emerge as you become clearer on your potential direction. Your list may get longer as the process evolves and before long you have enough information to make good decisions. You now know what matters to you. You've done that work in the earlier chapters. This is how to apply what you've learned.

Researching

- Ensure you've made a list of the information you need to gather and people to contact for each potential option. Be as specific as possible about what you need to find out.
- Find out where you can get the information that you need and set up a time line by which

you want to gather the information in order to keep moving forward. Use on-line sources, your career and personal networks and information specialists. Make action steps for each. Even small steps count.
- Assign time frames and goals to keep you on track. As you accomplish each item, tick it off and add more steps along the way as things emerge. The task is not to complete the list but to acquire the information you need and that may take you on some important detours.

For example, you may need to find guidelines on applying for your government pension, rules for health care coverage if you'll be away part of the year, the age at which you can qualify for reduced tuition for a program of study, or the climate of a place you're considering relocating to. It might be concrete or subjective information. Do you like living in a smaller center or what is it like to work where you would have less responsibility? Often where bureaucracy is involved the lead time to get the information may be longer than you'd expect.

I wanted to stay home for my children when they were young, yet not abandon my career so I did related volunteer work and occasional consulting. Before the children got into school I started to broadly consider the career area that I might return to. I divided a notebook into the three potential career areas I wanted to explore and brainstormed. Through networking over several months I amassed a long list of further things to find out under those three categories. I attended a career workshop and worked through a book on making career choices.

From what I knew of my values and temperament I decided on the questions I needed to get answered. These included how I could best balance my roles as a wife and mother of young children with a career in those areas, the nature of the work itself, and how I could grow in and with the field.

Through contacts and cold calls I discovered that in my field of interest a master's degree was becoming required. I knew I would need to study in my own city due to family obligations, so I interviewed professors at the schools and talked to colleagues who had taken the programs. The month after I got accepted into graduate school for my three year "transition plan" towards full time employment, magic happened. My previous employer called and offered me a promotion and perfect role that I'd dreamed of seven years earlier. I took the job, did school part-time and made arrangements for the children that minimized the disruption to them. Life happens to you while you're making other plans!

Always keep in mind what will work for you going forward, but don't discount new ideas too quickly. It may take a different form but be ideal. Trust the process of exploration. It may be that a previous dream or regret you had just won't work due to your age, resources or some other circumstance, but maybe some part of it being included in your life would be positive. You may not race motorcycles anymore, as you had dreamt of doing, but you may make artistic models of them, or attend motorcycle races, or volunteer on the marketing committee for races in your community. Or even find another sport you can do for adventure if that is what is underneath your dream.

Let's say that you want to relocate. Do you know the value of your current property and that of properties in the prospective community? Perhaps subscribe to a community newspaper ahead, to learn about local issues. Are there laws or extra expenses or implications that you need to consider, especially if it is in another jurisdiction? If you're investing in a second property, have you considered the tax and estate implications? Should you visit there on a trial basis or during various seasons in order to test the match with your preferences? A married couple I know with one person American by birth and the other Canadian had lots to explore. What are the implications on each of their citizenships and health benefits and government pensions of their decision of where to live? These are not reasons to not proceed, just to get organized and start researching.

Reality Checking

It can be challenging to accept what you discover and not to stubbornly hold onto what you want to hear. We need to let ourselves be confused in order to grow towards our future.

By reality checking I mean that you check your assumptions and compare information that you discover against such things as your "must haves", financial implications, and the cost and time involved to fulfill your idea. I'm not trying to lead you towards an unrealistic future or a situation where you put your security or relationships at risk. Keep checking in with your inner reactions as you proceed.

If you're considering a new type of work or turning your skill set into a consulting or entrepreneurial venture, then you may want to talk to people who have done so or shadow someone or take a part-time job to try it out, in addition to gathering legal implications. Notice how you feel when they're describing their activities. Could you arrange to take a sabbatical or leave from your workplace in order to test the waters on your comfort doing what you think want you do in retirement? If you're moving towards consulting, plan some lead time to get your materials and website started.

When I decided that I wanted to spend time on the west coast, I turned it into a fun project. I bought books and maps of the area and used the internet to research the climate, activities, house prices, travel hubs and work possibilities. I signed up for a weeklong workshop with like-minded people and planned a vacation in the vicinity. Friends connected me with people who lived there who generously shared their knowledge and connections. Because I'd done the work to confirm what mattered to me as I talked to people in coffee shops, real estate people and explored areas to check out my assumptions, my antenna were up to take in new information. I ended up in a different location and type of accommodation than I had expected, due to what I discovered. As you obtain realistic information continue to note what excites you the most and get ready to make more specific plans.

Planning

Planning is the cognitive process of thinking about the activities required in order to create a desired future. It includes developing, refining and integrating it in your life. It involves setting action steps, assigning timelines and following through. You get clearer and additional steps emerge as you spiral up and down through the research and reality checking activities. Some people gravitate more naturally to this activity than others. Here's an example of a couple, who started planning very early:

Diane, a professor and her husband Richard, an artist, had a long-term plan they conceived in their early 40s. They bought a property in France, renovated it over the years and explored the community during a couple of sabbaticals and summers and rented it out for many years. Their goal was to have it paid for and ready for their dream of living in Europe six months a year when they leave full-time employment. They planned far ahead and it paid off for them.

Michael and Kayla met on the west coast in the 1970s, but spent their adult lives in the east. They decided they wanted to return to the beauty and pace of the west. Five years before leaving full-time work they started vacationing there in different seasons to get a sense of the weather. Trying out various communities and activities to ensure it was right for them. They read bulletin boards in coffee shops and community centers to get a sense of the area. They planned for a period of transition when they sold their house, and rented in both the city they were leaving and the new city for a while, in order to have time to get rid of possessions, fulfill work obligations and get established in the new community. Michael may do some part-time teaching to earn extra money in order for them to travel as frequently as they would like.

> *How do you get organized?*
> *Who or what will keep you on track?*
> *What causes you to get off track?*

When my son was studying overseas a few years ago I used the stop-over rules with airline reward points to combine a visit with him, a business colleague in London and an old friend in Stockholm. In addition to wonderful social times and meaningful reunions, it integrated aspects of learning, fun, and adventure. The point is that you need to proactively generate the options plus be open to the opportunities in order to maximize how your interests and priorities can come together.

Some people I've coached carve out a dedicated time slot every week to keep moving their project along. Just do it! No one else cares as much as you do about your future. Remember how you felt when you dreamed your ideal future? Can you recapture that feeling or find a concrete symbol or image that would motivate you?

Role modeled by my mother, I've had strengths as a planner that serve me well. I've also learned as I've matured how important it is to hold a plan lightly, inviting the detours and surprises. When my marriage ended and there was much uncertainty, I kept as many doors open as possible. I bought in a demand area on transit so that if needed I could rent out a room or sell it. Have a plan B as well as a plan A. We can't control life and may end up with a plan G, but you have better chances of making change if you've considered worst case scenarios too.

As you research and reality check you'll keep spiraling back around and make many decisions. Keep organized. Our best decisions involve considered rational thought plus honored feelings and values. Remember what's most important to you for your future and what your decision making strengths and weaknesses are.

Use your skills to become the project manager of this venture. Treat it with the same respect that you would a work project. What's worked for you in the past to keep honest with your timelines and need to research details? If that's one of your strengths, then go to it. If you haven't had success in the past, then you might have some ideas as to why from the common barriers section of the next chapter. This is another time to consider working with a life coach or other professional. You may want to post your steps around your home to keep them visible, or check-in on them monthly when you pay bills. Or you may set aside a vacation period if you're still working, and focus just on that. Keep organized and keep your contact numbers in one place. Use a spread sheet if that's easier for you. Break the tasks down into manageable chunks and work your way through it. Enjoy the journey.

Who, or what, will support you?

- engage with people who are optimistic and proactive about their lives and want you to live your own best life as they'll keep you honest and encourage you
- have someone to check in with or contract with someone to help you keep on track with your research and prompt you on things you may have overlooked
- if you work best independently, what will get and keep you motivated and organized?

Expect, welcome, and reframe the unexpected

Remember that the goal is not to blindly carry out your plan but to stay open to what you learn as you head in that direction and modify as you gather more information. The goal is that you end up with the best choice for the next chapter of your life.

Your preferred options are a direction, or intent. The more that you've captured the essence of your dream, the better chance that you'll be successful in attaining it and also have the confidence to take the first step, even if the opportunity comes unexpectedly.

Lois and David were both conscientious about their financial planning in their adult lives and had planned to travel extensively in retirement. When David's job was eliminated unexpectedly in their early 50s, they seized the opportunity. Lois left her job and they traveled around the world for a year before transitioning to consulting roles. Because they had started to envision their future and had begun to prepare financially, this was possible. If the consulting activities don't work out they will look for occasional work or contracts.

Peter, a previous small business owner and entrepreneur and *Ruth*, a consultant, both in their mid-60s, are examples of a couple open to opportunities for their future. Completely by chance, Ruth encountered a young man in a grocery store in Northern Ontario and talked with him for five minutes about an interesting project he had started. Four months later, after a second meeting in Toronto, the couple committed to sponsoring a three-room school in Central America. They are now planning to travel to help build a school and in preparation they have started Spanish lessons. They look forward to a time in the winter to be in a warm climate helping to make a difference in the lives of the young children in the area. Since that initial conversation they have started reading about the many different ways that people in various countries are getting involved in moving beyond their geographical boundaries and have encouraged others to get involved in a continuing dialogue focusing on world issues.

Reframe

When I bought my first house I made a list of "must haves" and "nice to haves." One of my non-essential wishes was to have an arched doorway. I didn't get that but when I created my garden a few years later I took the opportunity to include and plan it around an arched arbor. I got a lot of pleasure in every season by starting and ending my day by looking out at it. Watch for opportunities to weave what matters to you, however inconsequential it may seem, into your life.

Don't let life be an either-or experience; get creative with options. If you stay open, they may come your way. If you tend to get discouraged at the first sign of the unexpected, acknowledge that about yourself and learn to take a deep breath to keep your energy up or engage in self-talk to view the situation from a different perspective. Learning how to reframe situations can be a handy life skill and I've found that I've become more resilient the more I've used it.

It may be impossible to do something that would have been a dream for you 20 or even 10 years ago. If that's the case and the dream still matters to you, then reframe the dream. You may have wanted to be a veterinarian but find that owning a dog or walking dogs as a part-time job gives you pleasure.

Reorient the dream; don't give up having one. You may not write a novel but write articles in a newsletter, not coach in the NHL but help in a children's sports league.

I know that I've said this but it bears repeating: we often don't believe deep down that we're entitled to live our ideal lives. Fear of success or failure or not feeling worthy can hold us back. You can still say no to an option or modify it, but if you never try, you'll not know what is possible.

I found a letter recently that I'd written to myself on the night of Canada's Centennial in 1967. I wrote of my dreams, challenges and cautions to myself. I started early to frame life as an opportunity for growth. I now understand both that we have less control than I had thought that night at age 17 and that magic and synchronicity can offer us an even fuller life if we're open to it. Controlled expectations are over-rated. However, having a considered dream to aspire to can pull us in a direction and serve to remind us of what's important to us. One way we learn to live with authenticity is by listening to and letting our values guide our decisions.

Sometimes my planning revolved around managing logistics and at other times in my life the vantage was to fill a void, or keep growing. Hold your plans lightly, yet work to make them happen. Be resilient enough to trust that you can reframe or modify them if necessary.

The important step is to become clear about what is at the core of your dream. Once you get to the motivational, emotional component, then the mystery is solved. I know in working with my clients that this is the key. There can be many alternatives that satisfy us once that aspect becomes clear. Frederic Hudson mentored us as professional coaches:

> *Lean into the wind and let our dreams pull us. It's important to have our clients get in touch with the feelings of their dream, not just running from the darkness of the present.*

Part Three

Making it Happen

Chapter 7

Overcoming Challenges

Avoiding pitfalls and transitioning well

*The gift of being honest in the review of our past
is to become aware of where we thrive
and where we get stuck in our lives.
Life does not require perfection of us
but rather authenticity and courage.*

STEP SIX is to address the things you can do to increase your chances of attaining your personal version of success. We'll see where your plan might go off track, what you can do about that and look at how to embrace periods of change and transition.

What allows you to keep moving towards achieving the things that really matter to you? It isn't always easy. Being honest with where you hold yourself back is one place to start. We think of barriers being imposed on us from outside, but many of the challenges come from within. Luckily they're the aspects over which you have most control.

You gain control by addressing those challenges starting with going deeper and discovering what's blocking you or interfering with your progress. Once you discover your part in the patterns, you can choose to take responsibility for that, see what you can learn and fulfill your plan successfully. We'll look at:

Common challenges
Hints and suggestions
Change and transitions

You may be tempted to rush past this section. I caution you to check it out carefully. I'm integrating what I've learned from years of experience and working with hundreds of clients. You may have a grandiose dream of reinventing yourself or a finely tuned one of the status quo on a smaller scale, but you owe it to yourself to start being honest with where you tend to let yourself down.

Acknowledging that you can let yourself down doesn't invite you to beat yourself up. Nor is this a time to be defensive. All of us will find at least one of our tendencies here. It's about claiming your pattern so that you can deal with it and make success more possible.

Common challenges

Procrastinating, denying, failing to plan

Being stuck in "if only"

Having a dream that isn't large or motivational enough, isn't yours, or is outdated

Having an unrealistic dream beyond your skill set or resources

Failing to trust that your realistic dream can come true

Failing to check out your assumptions and beliefs or being impulsive

Having an unhealthy need to control

Procrastinating, denying, failing to plan

In career transition coaching, when someone lost their job I always asked if they were surprised. Sometimes it was a shock, but people usually said they saw the signs of this possibility but didn't want to believe it. It was rare that they had started to consider options or update their resume.

The same can be true in a significant mid-career change or retirement if you haven't yet ascertained your financial circumstances for example. Have you started to plan for it? This isn't my area of expertise, but I'd recommend, if you haven't done so, you get a realistic view of your financial situation so you can maximize your alternatives and make the most accurate decisions for yourself. Many fail to get a true reading on their financial state of affairs or to open the discussion about personal preferences with their spouse. Is that true for you? What is holding you back?

What would it take to wake you up to your life – a serious disease, a heart attack, the breakdown of your relationship? Even with these crises some people prefer to ignore what's really happening or that time is running out. Look back at your review activities in chapter four and see what has prompted you to make changes in the past. Did you initiate changes proactively or in response to something imposed on you? How is this pattern relevant for you now?

Being stuck in "if only"

There are many excuses that we give ourselves to explain why we haven't succeeded in ways that matter to us. Anything will do – things about your family, childhood, birth order, appearance, the place where you grew up, your parents' divorce, to name a few. What do you repeat to yourself when you're defending why you didn't succeed at something? The caution is that you may use the same excuses for not reaching your "next step" dreams too.

Sometimes a client will describe a turning point from twenty or more years ago that goes something like this: "If only I'd studied psychology rather than engineering, I'd be happier in my job". They're holding onto that as a reason for life being less full than it could be. Are you telling yourself anything today to explain why you are not exactly where you wanted to be?

If what's holding you back relates to a person, then try and close that chapter of your life. If possible get together with them for a frank talk. Write a forgiveness letter or letter of appreciation if the person won't see you, isn't capable of emotional connection or is deceased. The goal is to move beyond whatever is holding you back. You may want to write it to yourself, acknowledging that you did the best you could at the time. It's especially important that we say and do what matters most to us so that we don't have regrets. You want to enter this next significant period of your life as free of baggage as you can be, giving yourself permission to open to possibilities.

You may have something that has genuinely proven a challenge in your life. Own your sadness and any flashbacks you have of events or circumstances. Explore it through therapy if you need to, but attempt to move into, through, and beyond it. Why pay an even higher price and carry that burden with you? There are numerous inspirational stories of people who have overcome huge odds. Reading biographies of successful people can inspire you to embrace life fully. The goal is to let your old story line and excuses go and replace them with your new future.

Having a dream that isn't large or motivational enough, isn't yours, or is outdated

At what point do you pull back and reach for something less than you could be or for something that fails to motivate you? You may be leading what seems to be a charmed life, but inside feel empty. What's that about? Often when we're not fully present in our own lives we're not aware that we're just going through the motions and that time is slipping by. Until you let yourself feel that, it won't go away but will nag at you in disguised ways, perhaps through emotional or physical health challenges. The key is to go inside; get in touch with yourself at a deep level. Activities such as yoga, journaling, meditation, body work or attending a workshop for personal renewal are a few ways to explore and update your personal dream.

Your future is already happening, whether you're engaged in guiding the direction and maximizing the opportunities that present, or not. Are you still holding onto a dream of what you thought the perfect job or your perfect retirement would be all about when you started on your adult journey? Is your dream outdated for who you are now or for your circumstances? In what way is it not reflective of who you know yourself to be at this juncture, how the world has changed, or in what matters to you?

Having an unrealistic dream beyond your skill set or resources

What's your track record of achieving the goals that you set for yourself? Do you set unrealistic goals such as those requiring skills or resources far beyond what you could ever attain? Sometimes people do this in order to give themselves permission to not set goals that require specific actions of them, in case they fail. Those who fear success on some level may not want to set a realistic goal in case they can't achieve it.

Realistic goals allow you to stretch yourself or think long-term and fill in action steps along the way to plot a path that has a probability of success. Our dreams take place in the context of our times and circumstances, so we need to keep in touch with those realities.

If you tend to be unrealistic or impulsive, then you might want to be especially careful. How much time do you have left for re-training? Does your dream involve a physical strength that you may not have as you age? Explore how your financial situation impacts your dream.

If you start planning early enough you can set aside savings, learn a required skill, attain a certification or know what you need to do to increase your chances of success.

Several participants in my research were already contributing to, or expecting to be financially responsible for parents. Women expected to outlive their spouse, resulting in being without their partner at a vulnerable older age. This is a consideration for both men and women due to the potential for increased longevity.

Failing to trust that your realistic dream can come true

Frequently in my consulting practice we'll work at in-depth assessment and exploration of someone's profile, they will do reality checking in their network and get to what they say would be the perfect type of job for them. Then they'd say, "Oh, I'll never be able to find that". Why?

It could be that you lack confidence or have a pessimist attitude about life. Or you may not have experience being proactive as you had a career or life circumstance where you let fate or others be in charge. Have you let life come to you or have you gone after it? Or was your life a bit of both? Some of us don't feel that we deserve our life to be full.

Why would you not be worthy of living the life you want to have? Do you believe that your actions can influence the outcome you want or do you feel more of a victim of circumstances? This tends to be a life view that evolves over time, either positively or negatively impacting us. This attitude can be tricky to change but, being aware that you're contributing to that barrier is important to acknowledge even if you just loosen your grip a bit and trust that good things can happen.

Failing to check out your assumptions and beliefs or being impulsive

When I ask people why an option wouldn't work for them, their answer is often based on their assumptions. Some individuals want to have things settled so much that they can be impulsive, or make decisions without sufficient information. They don't see what might be possible. It can also be due to a lack of confidence, or a way to stay safe from taking risks, but if there's really something you want to have happen, then you might need to be courageous and do some research.

To make good decisions, you may want to try new behaviors. Talk to people, ask open questions and listen to their experience with your own criteria and lens. Someone else's worst case scenario may be your best due to differences in personality or preferences. Some people would be lonely retiring to a small cottage town while others would be happier. Stay open to things that you have never considered as you do your research and planning.

Having an unhealthy need to control

When I was young I thought that if I did everything "right" then life would be smooth sailing. It wouldn't be a normal life if we didn't encounter challenges to our dreams along the way. Accepting our impermanence and the underlying lack of control in the existential human condition is a reality to befriend. Find your own comfortable yet courageous balance between trusting possibility and engaging in what needs to be attended to.

I tend to look long-term and make my best decisions by gathering information and trying possibilities. No one has all the information, and sometimes overdoing that activity becomes a reason not to act in a timely way. Being resilient and trusting that I can survive adversity allows me to live life lighter, be less controlling, and be more in flow. It isn't as easy as it sounds, but if you can hold that belief as a central core to return to, you can become more comfortable with the feeling of lack of control along the way.

If you've been successful in your career you may have been skilled at controlling things. Once outside an organizational structure and bottom-line orientation being able to realize that we can't control everything we may wish to, is a maturing life skill. Some people learn that early in life and some never do. Have you learned that yet?

Hints and suggestions

- Prepare an inventory of your successes. What life skills and qualities do you bring to make your dreams come true? Think of a time when you set a goal for yourself and achieved it. What did you do that promoted its success? On a practical level, if you're working, keep your resume and network up to date.

- Surround yourself with people who do make their dreams come true. If there aren't any in your circle of friends and family, then consciously seek them out through activities, groups and causes that attract such people.

- To move towards your goals and keep your personal barriers to success in mind, ask what you need to start, keep, and stop doing.

- If you tend to set unrealistic dreams, explore what's underneath that dream. You may not be able to be a rock star, but perhaps you can attend more concerts, learn an instrument, join or lead a fan club. In other words "reframe" what's possible. Maybe it's about adventure or performing more than the music for you? Get at what that dream represents for you.

- If you're faced with a health condition or illness that precludes you doing what you wanted at this stage of life, find a way to do whatever you can. You can prepare a video or journal as a legacy, or proactively move into a living space that maximizes your comfort and options.

- If lack of structure, or the unknown, is uncomfortable for you, and that's a reason for you being stuck, then make up a plan in order to control what you can. Establish a routine, decide how many changes you make concurrently, or make a long transition plan.
- Get over the regrets by reflecting backwards, but living forwards and honoring your feelings in the present.
- Become aware of where in your body you feel it when you start to get scared. Your body is giving you information constantly – listen to it.
- Establish a way to keep in touch with your genuine wishes and preferences: journaling, meditation, workshops or retreats, hiring a personal coach. Anything that makes this a priority so you keep living your own best life.
- Ask yourself what would happen if you "went for it," and didn't "achieve it"?
- What scares you most about the next stage of your life or your retirement?

Activity

Considering the challenges above, identify the ones that you struggle with most, revisit your plan and add any steps, or make any changes to the plan that might maximize your personal success.

Change and transitions

Life is change. If your plan is to leave your current career and head in a new direction, expect a time of exploration and transition. If you're leaving full-time work, then your role, finances, status, how you spend your time, how much time you can share with your spouse, family and friends, how you see yourself and are seen by the community may all change. Change invites possibility. Depending on your situation this could be positive or negative experience. We're vulnerable and open to new things as we transition and our plan rolls out. Trust your intuition during your transition and don't be afraid to claim when others ask you, that "I'm not sure yet."

When you explore "what if?" it's as if a wave picks you up off your ground and you let yourself be carried for a while. You don't need to struggle to get back to the same shore. There are always new shores. A friend said to me when I hit a low point in the midst of riding on my wave, "you have to expect the odd face-plant." Be kind to yourself, open to supportive people and allow time for your transition and renewal.

Nature has cycles of renewal. So does human history. I saw an image while visiting Dubrovnik, Croatia in 2003 that has stayed with me. Inside the walled mediaeval town, beside a huge drawbridge at the entrance, there was a street map of the city showing the numerous houses that had been bombed during the war only a decade earlier. Within the walls on the cobbled streets shiny from centuries of human use, retailers were again thriving and student artists were selling their paintings to tourists. The transition of renewal was under-way.

Times of transition are fertile opportunities for growth. They allow you to reflect on your life, start to give up what isn't relevant anymore, and reclaim what's most important to you. This reflecting is like the first activity of a transition, or what Bridges, who has written extensively on the topic of change, calls the "endings." He suggests that you let go of attachment to your current reality before you move into your future. He also recommends that you identify yourself with the final result of the new beginning. Bridges sees change as a situational reality and transition as a psychological re-orientation.[1]

How to thrive during transitions

Transition is a normal part of the change process. Expect it. I've seen people do this very successfully. I suggest that you include it as a step in your plan. You can use it as a time to unwind, do things that you've put off, reconnect with people, learn new skills or invite pleasure or exercise into your life in a more meaningful way.

I encourage you to mark and celebrate your transition in some way: with a party, growing a beard or trying a new hairstyle. Let go of the old, and open to the new. Open to the unexpected synchronicities and people who enter your life to enrich it.

- Ask what you expect to miss about your current reality. Perhaps you can build an aspect of that into your new life if you get underneath to what you value. For example if you fear that you'll miss the structured nature of your career life, build a new routine into your life.

- Even if the new is something you want, you may still feel some discomfort at the beginning and it's healthy to acknowledge that.
- Get rid of concrete things you're finished with in order to make room for the new. This could be books, clothes, old technology, hobbies you won't do again.
- Celebrate endings in order to let go of the past.
- Be intentional and ritualize new events.
- Make your own symbols. They can give you leverage, make the experience deeper, get to what is underneath a motivation for your new dream, or give you the answer as to why you are holding on to something.
- If you're considering moving to a new community, consider renting to try it out first.
- Set a routine for yourself, if that was something you liked about working. Acknowledge what you benefited from during your working life. Make lists of what you will miss and not miss.
- Claim where you actually are and own the being in-between by assuming a time of adjustment as the normal thing it is.
- Grieve the loss of the familiar in what you're about to change in your life – people, security, status, routine, not taking responsibility for your unhappiness. Letting go and grieving is a normal part of the process. We know that is true for our relation-

ship with the people who pass through and out of our lives. It's also true for the roles we have played and activities that we have invested our life in.

Activities

Letting go

What did you find out about yourself in the review activities about how you experience transitions? How do you do endings? Do you hold on too long, or never look back?

Acknowledge your feelings or they will get in the way without you knowing it. Even if you are not an emotional type of person try and ascertain how you feel about the changes.

In what way has your career journey or life let you down?

In what way did it surpass your expectations, or surprise you?

If you had to do it again, what would you want more of?

What price do you pay for your personality style?

What are you looking forward to the most?

What are you worst and best case scenarios of how your plan will evolve?

There's no one way to be successful. Use who you are, and what has brought you success with change in the past. There's a continuum of how people relate to change and deal with transitions. Which of these is most like you?

- Do you like change and enthusiastically invite it into your life? Do you become easily bored and are you continuously changing things?
- Do you throw your net wide hoping to capture many possibilities and then creatively integrate them?
- Are you matter of fact, preferring to be rational and focus on facts rather than how you feel about things?

Transition can feel uncomfortable, but it's a necessary and normal part of most change. I know from personal experience how complex, challenging and rewarding transitions can be. Don't get stalled, but don't short-change yourself by grasping at a new life too quickly. The potential depths of our major life transitions are opportunities to learn who we really are, grow, heal, and be authentic and courageous. A day will come when you will *know* that you've arrived at your next destination...for the time being.

Chapter 8

Living Your Dream

If not now – then when?

*Learn to make the most of life,
make glad each passing day,
for life will never bring you back
the chances swept away.*

The advice in the above quote, that I was given as a child, is even more relevant to me in mid-life. Our life experience offers each of us opportunities to learn lessons on how to really live and junctures that invite us to create possibilities. STEP SEVEN is to live life fully and courageously, embracing what you believe in. The wisdom that I claim from my journey so far gives me peace, pause, and a sense of impatience.

I believe that:

*We are each responsible for our own life choices
We need to wake up and live authentically and fully
We need to think outside the box and stretch ourselves
We need to do it now*

Invitation

A few years ago I attended a program with approximately 45 mainly mid-life men and women from Canada, the United States, and the United Kingdom who aspired to be leaders by coaching in our areas of expertise. The group included consultants, doctors, executives, entrepreneurs, lawyers, scientists and others interested in adult transformation and renewal. We were challenged to dream impactful dreams, be honest in our communication, trust, and live courageously.

The forum provided an opportunity to discover where we get stuck and hone techniques to get back on track. Over the course of the nine months we had parents die, people lost their jobs, got promoted, relocated, grandchildren were born, my long-term marriage ended, and someone was diagnosed with a major health issue. Life happened. In a supportive learning community we continued to admit when we were outside our comfort zone and to keep stretching to reach our dreams.

Weeks before we were to fly from our various locations through Los Angeles to Santa Barbara, to reconvene, the terrorist attacks of September 11, 2001 occurred. One group member was head of human resources for a major US airline and was thrown into handing the impact of increased security. Another was an executive at a multi-national in New Jersey who was dealing with deep loss and confusion, and fear of flying only a month after having lost employees and friends. Within days we gathered as a group on a conference call to share our reactions and deal with concerns regarding whether to cancel the upcoming travel.

We had let ourselves be known to each other due to the nature of the program and depth of our interpersonal communication, which meant that sharing the impact of the tragedy, was powerful. Despite some individuals having been directly impacted and many of us feeling nervous about flying, the course was held and we all showed up. "Showing up" courageously for what matters to us in our life is what is required of us. Don't try to be someone you're not, but implement a plan for your future that suits your bravest self. The good news is that once you wake up and live your life mindful of your feelings and actions, you may never go back to making excuses for not living your best life.

The more I've discovered the ways I hold myself back and have embraced change, the more fully I'm living. My learning has been to be honest with my weaknesses, own my strengths, breathe, and just keep going. I'm not always able to do so, but when I do, it's a freeing, healthy and successful way to live.

What were your dreams for yourself and the world as you became an adult? Were you involved in anti-war protests, championing the space program, fighting for women's rights, civil rights, or raising environmental concerns? Is there a place for that enthusiasm and passion in your next chapter? This book has been about your personal process, but as I said at the beginning, we live our lives in the context of our times. These are challenging times. What does your world and your next life chapter require of you?

Create and implement your plan as boldly as you can. Craft it so that it is yours. I invite, or perhaps challenge you to consider finding a cause that matters to you, and find a way to show up. In what way can you keep your life relevant and both live, and leave, this world in peace? The world needs all of us – the best in us, living in flow and with purpose.

What can your life be again?
What can your life finally be?
What can your life be next?

Namaste

Notes

Acknowledgements

1. Kornfield, J. (1993). *A path with heart: A guide through the perils and promises of spiritual life.* New York: Bantam Books.

Introduction

1. Foot, D.K. (1996). *Boom, Bust & Echo: How to profit from the coming demographic shift.* Toronto, ON: Macfarlane Walter & Ross. pp. 18-22.
2. 2006 Census, Statistics Canada: the actual total of males and females is 10,018,010. The number of Canadians in that group ages 55-64 jumped by 28 per cent over five years to 3.7 million, said Statistics Canada, citing the 2006 census.

Chapter Two

1. Dychtwald, K. (1999). *Age Power: How the 21st Century will be ruled by the new old.* New York: Jeremy P. Tarcher/Putnam. p. xix. Dychtwald sets out the aging related dangers as well as offering preventative solutions.
2. Frederic Hudson is the co-founder of The Hudson Institute of Santa Barbara, California, specializing in renewal, coaching and leadership training. I attended

the Institute in 2000-2001 and refer to Frederic's wisdom in this book.

3. The audio programs *A Special Place: Self-esteem and Relaxation Techniques for Children*, and *Time Out! Problem-solving and Stress Management for Teenagers* are both available for download from my website www.lifedesignconsultants.com

4. Weil, A. (2005). *Healthy aging: A lifelong guide to your physical and spiritual well-being.* New York: Alfred A. Knopf, Inc. I attended his workshop on Integrative Medicine on Cortes Island, British Columbia in 2006. www.hollyhock.ca.

5. There are several books that have informed my thinking on this over the past 20 years, starting with: Wilber, K. (Ed.). (1982). *The Holographic Paradigm and other paradoxes: Exploring the leading edge of science.* Boston, MA: New Science Library; Grof, S. with H.Z. Bennett. (1993). *The Holotrophic Mind: The three levels of human consciousness and how they shape our lives.* New York: HarperCollins Publishers; and most recently Schwartz, G.E. with Simon, W.L. (2007). *The Energy Healing Experiments: Science reveals our natural power to heal.* New York: Simon & Schuster, Inc.

6. There are numerous books being released on healthy aging. A few resources are: Roizen, M.F. (1999). *RealAge: Are you as young as you can be?* New York: HarperCollins Publishers Inc.; Rowe, J.W. & Kahn, R.L. (1998). *Successful Aging.* New York: Pantheon Books; and Weil, A. (2005). *Healthy aging: A lifelong guide to your physical and spiritual well-being.* New York: Alfred A. Knopf, Inc.

7. Allen Tough's *Expand your life: A pocket book for personal change,* written in 1980 – College Entrance

Examination Board, New York is out of print, but he indicated that it is still in circulation. He's an internationally respected futurist and leader in adult learning projects. www.allentough.com

8. Reiner, S. & Moll, C. (2005) "Leisure development and planning throughout the lifespan and its implications on life satisfaction in older adults." Presentation at the American Counseling Association Convention in Atlanta, Georgia.

9. Rollins, J. (2005, Aug.) Living a life of leisure: All work and no play? How leisure participation affects life satisfaction. *Counseling Today*, 10-11.

10. Frankl, V.E. (2006). *Man's search for meaning.* Boston, MA: Beacon Press.

11. Bettis, B. (2001, July). The Hudson Institute of Santa Barbara Newsletter.

12. Moen, P., Erickson, W.A., Agarwal, M., Fields, V., Todd, L. (2000). *The Cornell retirement and well-being study: Final report.* Ithaca, NY: Bronfenbrenner Life Course Center, Cornell University.

13. Freidan, B. (1993). *The fountain of age.* New York: Simon & Schuster, p. 159.

Chapter Three

1. Clemes, L.D. – see Treleaven, L.D. Clemes. (1999). Mid-life professional women envisage retirement: aspirations, attitudes and concerns. (Doctoral dissertation, University of Toronto, 1999). *Dissertation Abstracts International, A 60/08,* p. 2768. A literature review, especially of studies related to women is found in chapter two of the dissertation.

2. Quoted in Sheehy, G. (1995). *New passages: Mapping your life across time.* Toronto: Random House of Canada Limited, p. 5, from the author's interview with Dr. Kenneth Manton a Demographer at Duke University.
3. Growe, S.J. (2003, December 8). Uniting generations will improve the quality of life. *Toronto Star,* p. E7.
4. Korn/Ferry International & University of California, Los Angeles, Anderson Graduate School of Management. (1993). *Decade of the Executive Woman.* New York: Korn/Ferry International.
5. Clemes, L.D. – see Treleaven, L.D. Clemes. (1999). Mid-life professional women envisage retirement: aspirations, attitudes and concerns. (Doctoral dissertation, University of Toronto, 1999). *Dissertation Abstracts International, A 60/08,* p. 2768. Data on women's views on retirement were almost non-existent when I undertook my research in 1997. My dissertation was among the first qualitative studies to research that question with the generation of women, then ages 45-54. It was novel to consider that retirement was being "reinvented." I've continued to do informal research with men, as well as women, and to follow emerging societal and workplace trends. Research aims to expand our understanding, in a focused way, so I chose to look at the true pioneers of that generation – the professional women.
6. Brehony, K.A. (1996). *Awakening at mid-life: A guide to reviving your spirit, recreating your life and returning to your truest self.* New York: Riverhead Books, p. 5.
7. Betty Freidan (1921-2006) a feminist, explored a broad sampling of men and women, then 50 years of age and older for her 1993 book, *The fountain of age,* and found an increasing diversity in life patterns. She presents an optimistic look at mid-life and beyond.

8. Eichler, M. (1997). *Family shifts: Families, policies and gender equality.* Don Mills, ON: Oxford University Press, p. 36.
9. Griggs, S. & Wright, S. (2001, Spring). Dowagers and dreams: Coaching women's later career stages. *Career Planning and Adult Development Journal, 17*(1) 17.
10. Statistics Canada. 2007. Age Groups (13) and Sev (3) for the Population of Caada, Provinces and Territories, 1921 to 2006 Censuses – 100% Data (table). Topic-based tabulation. 2006 Census of Population. Statistics Canada cataologue no. 97-551-XCB2006005. Ottawa. Released July 17, 2007.
11. Marshall, K. & Ferrao, V. (August 2007). "Participation of older workers." Statistics Canada – PERSPECTIVES, Catalogue no. 75-001-XIE. Vol. 8(8), p. 1-11.
12. Greig, L.J.A. (2006, November). *Recent developments in Canadian laws affecting mature workers.* Presentation and materials delivered by Senior Associate, Osler, Hoskin & Harcourt LLP at Summit on the Mature Workforce, Toronto, Canada.
13. Gabliani, V.I. (1993) Retirement decision-making in married professional women: An application of the theory of planned behavior (Doctoral dissertation, Washington University, 1993). *Dissertation Abstracts International, B 55/02,* p.589.
14. Finlayson J. (1995). *Against the current: Canadian women talk about fifty years on the job.* Toronto: Doubleday, Canada.
15. Moen, P. et al. (2001). Couples' work/retirement transitions, gender, and marital quality. *Social Psychology Quarterly 64*(1), 55-71.

16. Karp, D.A. (1989). The social construction of retirement among professionals 50-60 years old. *The Gerontologist, 29,* 750-760.
17. Erdner, R.A. & Guy, R.F. (1990). Career identification and women's attitudes to retirement. *International Journal of Aging and Human Development, 30(2),* 129-139.
18. Sheehy, G. (2006). *Sex and the seasoned woman: Pursing the passionate life.* New York: Random House Inc.
19. Moen, P., Erickson, W.A., Agarwal, M., Fields, V., Todd, L. (2000). *The Cornell retirement and well-being study: Final report.* Ithaca, NY: Bronfenbrenner Life Course Center, Cornell University.
20. Haid, R. & Williams, C. (1999, Fall). Counseling for the Third Quarter of Life. *Career Planning and Adult Development Journal, 15*(3), 5-8. Richard Haid, Third Quarter of Life, www.adultmentor.com
21. Simon-Rusinowitz, L., Wilson, L., Marks, L., Krach, C. & Welch, C. (1998). Reconfiguring retirement for baby boomers. *Journal of Mental Health Counseling, 15,* 106-116.
22. Merril Lynch and Ken Dychtwald (2005) *The New Retirement Survey.* The survey took place in 2005 with 2,348 US adults ages 40-58 weighted to reflect the demographics by gender, race, region, education and household income.
23. Harris, R. (2004, July 12). The Boomers' Golden Age. *Marketing Magazine. Rogers Media Inc.*

Chapter Four

1. Bolen, J.S. (1994). *Crossing to Avalon: A woman's midlife pilgrimage.* New York: HarperSanFrancisco.

2. A career provides the opportunity to learn about and express who you are. From a constructivist career counseling theoretical perspective, it's purported that personal growth issues and themes in a person's life can be explored in the context of their career. Two articles by Savikas (1997, March), and one by Brott (2005, December) are referenced in the Additional Resources section and elaborate on this topic.
3. *Live Like You Were Dying*, sung by Tom McGraw, written by Tim Nichols, and Craig Wiseman. 2004.
4. Csikszentmihalyi, M. (1997). *Finding flow: The psychology of engagement with everyday life.* New York: Basic Books. This is an inspirational book to show you ways to find joy in complete engagement in ordinary activities. I experience this as similar to what Buddhists and meditation leaders call "being present" the powerful and healthy experience of surrendering worries of the future or regrets of the past and being with what is, in a given moment.
5. Weil, A. (2005). *Healthy aging: A lifelong guide to your physical and spiritual well-being.* New York: Alfred A. Knopf, Inc. pp. 234-238.

Chapter Five

1. Brunning, F. (2007, Spring). Retirement: How one litigator has redefined the concept. *The Advocates' E-Brief* 18(3) p. 22.
2. Hutching, P. & Elly Klimitz, B. (2004, December). Former surgeon teaching others in woodcarving craft. *Town Crier,* p.7.
3. Alphonso, C. (2004, June 11). He's a university grad – at 93. *The Globe & Mail,* pp. A1, A11.

4. Growe, S.J. (2005, June 25). Graduation at long last. *The Globe and Mail*, p. F6.
5. Foot, D.K. (1996). *Boom, Bust & Echo: How to profit from the coming demographic shift.* Toronto, ON: Macfarlane Walter & Ross, pp.39-40.

Chapter Seven

1. Bridges, W. (1980). *Transitions: Making sense of life's changes.* New York: Addison-Wesley Publishing Company, pp. 145-146. His distinction between change and transition was one that he shared in a teleconference I participated in March 2001 that was hosted by The Hudson Institute of Santa Barbara.

Additional Resources

The following are resources that have informed my thinking. It's not meant to be an exhaustive list. I share them for those who may be interested.

Mid-life, Finding Purpose, Renewal

Apter, T. (1995). *Secret paths: Women in the new mid-life.* New York: W.W. Norton & Company.

Bateson, M.C. (1990). *Composing a life.* New York: Penguin Books.

Bepko, C. & Krestan, J. (1993). *Singing at the top of our lungs: Women, love and creativity.* New York: HarperCollins Publishers, Inc.

Bolen, J.S. (1994). *Crossing to Avalon: A woman's mid-life pilgrimage.* New York: HarperSanFransisco.

Borysenko, J. (1993). *Fire in the soul: A new psychology of spiritual optimism.* New York: Warner Books, Inc.

Brehony, K.A. (1996). *Awakening at mid-life: A guide to reviving your spirit, recreating your life and returning to your truest self.* New York: Riverhead Books.

Frankl, V.E. (2006). *Man's search for meaning.* Boston, MA: Beacon Press.

Freidan, B. (1993). *The fountain of age.* New York: Simon & Schuster.

Hagberg, J. & Leider, R. (1988). *The Inventurers: Excursions in life and career renewal (3rd edition)*. Reading, MA: Addison-Wesley Publishing Company Inc.

Hollis, J. (2005). *Finding meaning in the second half of life*. New York: Gotham Books.

Houston, J. (1997). *A passion for the possible: A guide to realizing our true potential*. New York: HarperCollins Publishers, Inc.

Hudson, F.M. & McLean, P.D. (2000). *Lifelaunch: A passionate guide to the rest of your life, 3rd edition, revised*. Santa Barbara, CA: The Hudson Institute Press.

Leider, R.J. (1997). *The power of purpose: Creating meaning in your life and work*. San Francisco, CA: Berrett-Koehler Publishers, Inc.

Leider, R.J., & Shapiro, D.A. (2004). *Claiming your place at the fire: Living the second half of your life on purpose*. San Francisco, CA: Berrett-Koehler Publishers, Inc.

Levoy, G. (1997). *Callings: Finding and following an authentic life*. New York: Three Rivers Press.

Lloyd, C. (1997). *Creating a life worth living: A practical course in career design for artists, innovators and others aspiring to live a creative life*. New York: HarperCollins Publishers, Inc.

Murphy, J.S. & Hudson, F.M. (1995). *The joy of old: A guide to successful elderhood*. Altadena, CA: Geode Press.

Palmer, P.J. (2000). *Let your life speak: Listening to the voice of vocation*. San Francisco CA: Jossey-Bass Inc.

Pollan, S.M. & Levine, M. (2004). *Second acts: Creating the life you really want, building the career you truly desire*. New York: HarperCollins Publishers, Inc.

Rosenthal, M.S. (2000). *Women of the '60s turning 50*. Prentice Hall: Canada.

Schachter-Shalomi, Z. & Miller, R. (1995). *From Age-ing to Sage-ing: A profound new vision of growing older.* New York: Warner Books.

Schulman, A.K. (1995). *Drinking the rain.* New York: Penguin Books.

Sheehy, G. (1995). *New passages: Mapping your life across time.* Toronto: Random House of Canada Limited.

Sheehy, G. (1998). *Understanding men's passages: Discovering the new map of men's lives.* Toronto: Random House of Canada Limited.

Sheehy, G. (2006). *Sex and the seasoned woman: Pursuing the passionate life.* New York: Random House.

Sher, B. (1998). *It's only too late if you don't start now: How to create your second life after 40.* New York: Delacorte Press.

Personal Change

Bridges, W. (1980). *Transitions: Making sense of life's changes.* New York: Addison-Wesley Publishing Company.

Jeffers, S. (1987). *Feel the fear and so it anyway: Dynamic techniques for turning fear, indecision and anger into power, action and love.* New York: Ballantine Books.

Knaus, W.J. (1994). *Change your life now: Powerful techniques for positive change.* New York: John Wiley & Sons, Inc.

Kumar, S.M. (2005). *Grieving mindfully: A compassionate and spiritual guide to coping with loss.* Oakland, CA: New Harbringer Publications, Inc.

Kushner, H.S. (2001). *Living a life that matters: Resolving the conflict between conscience and success.* New York: Alfred A. Knopf.

Richo, D. (1999). *Shadow dance: Liberating the power & creativity of your dark side.* Boston, MA. Shambhala Publications Inc.

Societal Perspective

Dychtwald, K. (1999). *Age Power: How the 21st Century will be ruled by the new old.* New York: Jeremy P. Tarcher/ Putnam.

Finlayson J. (1995). *Against the current: Canadian women talk about fifty years on the job.* Toronto: Doubleday, Canada.

Foot, D.K. (1996). *Boom, bust & echo: How to profit from the coming demographic shift.* Toronto, ON: Macfarlane Walter & Ross.

Fox, M. (1994). *The reinvention of work: A new vision of livelihood for our time.* New York: HarperCollins Publishers, Inc.

Grof, S. with H. Z. Bennett. (1993*). The Holotrophic Mind: The three levels of human consciousness and how they shape our lives.* New York: HarperCollins Publishers.

Novelli, B. (Ed). & Workman, B. (2006). *50+: Igniting a revolution to reinvent America.* New York: St. Martin's Press.

Pink, D.H. (2005). *A whole new mind: Moving from the information age to the conceptual age.* New York: Riverhead Books.

Schellenberg, G. & Ostrovsky, Y. The retirement plans and expectations of older workers. 2007 General Social Survey Report. *Canadian Social Trends,* Statistics Canada – Catalogue no. 11-008, pp. 11-34.

Westley, F., Zimmerman, B. & Patton M. Q. (2006). *Getting to maybe: How the world is changed.* Random House Canada.

Wilber, K. (Ed.). (1982). *The Holographic Paradigm and other paradoxes: Exploring the leading edge of science.* Boston, MA: New Science Library.

Spiritual Perspective

Chodron, P. (1994). *Start where you are: A guide to compassionate living.* Boston, MA: Shambhala Publications, Inc.

Chodron, P. (1997). *When things fall apart: Heart advice for difficult times.* Boston, MA: Shambhala Publications, Inc.

Csikszentmihalyi, M. (1997). *Finding flow: The psychology of engagement with everyday life.* New York: Basic Books.

Farhi, D. (1996). *The breathing book: Good health and vitality through essential breath work.* New York: Henry Holt and Company.

Gendlin, E.T. (1981). *Focusing, second edition.* New York: Bantam Books.

Hart, W. (1987). *The art of living: Vipassana meditation as taught by S.N. Goenka.* New York: HarperCollins Publishers, Inc.

Kabat-Zinn, J. (1994). *Wherever you go, there you are: Mindfulness meditation in everyday life.* New York: Hyperion.

Kornfield, J. (1993). *A path with heart: A guide through the perils and promises of spiritual life.* New York: Bantam Books.

Salzberg, S. (2002). *Faith: trusting your own deepest experience.* New York: Riverhead Books.

Surya Das, Lama (2000). *Awakening the Buddhist heart: Integrating love, meaning and connection into every part of your life.* New York: Broadway Books.

The New Retirement

Anthony, M. (2006). *The new retire-mentality: Planning your life and living your dreams...at any age you want (second edition)*. Chicago, IL: Kaplan Publishing.

Bland, W. (2005). *Retire in style: 60 outstanding places across the USA and Canada*. Next Decade, Inc.

Cullinane, J. & Fitzgerald, C. (2006). *The new retirement: The ultimate guide to the rest of your life*. Rodale Inc. New York.

Saylor, D. & Heffington, G., with S. Marks. (2006). *Get inspired to retire: Over 150 ideas to help you find your retirement*. Chicago IL: Dearborn Trade Publishing.

Waxman, B., Mendelson, R. (eds.) (2006). *How to love your retirement*. Atlanta Georgia: Hundreds of Heads Books.

Well-Being

Caldwell, C. (1996). *Getting our bodies back; Recovery, healing and transformation through body-centered psychotherapy*. Boston, MA: Shambhala Publications, Inc.

Doidge, N. (2007). *The brain that changes itself*. Viking, USA.

Edwards, P., Lhotsky, M. & Turner, J. (1999). *The Healthy Boomer: A no-nonsense mid-life health guide for women and men*. Toronto, ON: McClelland & Stewart Inc.

Kabat-Zinn, J. (1990). *Full catastrophe living: Using the wisdom of your body and mind to face stress, pain, and illness*. New York: Dell Publishing.

Kuhl, D. (2002). *What dying people want: Practical wisdom for the end of life*. Doubleday Canada.

Mahoney, D. & Restak, R. (1998). *The longevity strategy: How to live to 100 using the brain-body connection.* Toronto, ON: John Wiley and Sons, Inc.

Maté, G. (2003). *When the body says no: The cost of hidden stress.* Toronto, ON: Alfred A. Knopf Canada.

Mayo Clinic (Creagon, E. T. Ed.) *Mayo Clinic on healthy aging: Answers to help you make the most of your life.* Rochester, MINN: Mayo Clinic Health Information.

Northrup, C. (2001). *The wisdom of menopause: Creating physical and emotional health and healing during the change.* New York: Bantam Books.

Nuland, S.B. (1993). *How we die: Reflections on life's final chapter.* New York: Random House.

Nuland, S.B. (2007). *The art of aging: A doctor's prescription for well-being.* New York: Random House.

Roizen, M.F. (1999). *Real age: Are you as young as you can be? An age reduction program that can make you live and feel up to 26 years younger.* New York: HarperCollins Publishers, Inc.

Rowe, J.W. & Kahn, R.L. (1998). *Successful aging: The MacArthur Foundation Study shows you how the lifestyle choices you make now – more than heredity – determine your health and vitality.* New York: Pantheon Books.

Schwartz, G.E. with Simon, W.L. (2007). *The energy healing experiments: Science reveals our natural power to heal.* New York: Simon & Schuster, Inc.

Shankle, W. Rodman & Amen, D.G. (2004). *Preventing Alzheimer's: Ways to help prevent, delay, detect and even halt Alzheimer's disease and other forms of memory loss.* New York: G.P. Putnam's Sons.

Vaillant, G.E. (2002). *Aging well: Surprising guideposts to a happier life from the landmark Harvard study of adult development.* Boston: Little, Brown and Company.

Weenolsen, P. (1996). *The art of dying: How to leave this world with dignity and grace, at peace with yourself and your loved ones.* New York: St. Martin's Press.

Weil, A. (1995). *Spontaneous healing: How to discover and enhance your body's natural ability to maintain and heal itself.* New York: Alfred A. Knopf, Inc.

Weil, A. (2005). *Healthy aging: A lifelong guide to your physical and spiritual well-being.* New York: Alfred A. Knopf, Inc.

Professional Journals and References

Alphonso, C. (2004, June 11). He's a university grad – at 93. *The Globe & Mail,* pp. A1, A11.

Blanchette, P., & Valcour, V. (1998). Health and aging among Baby Boomers. *Generations, 22(1),* 76-80.

Brott, P.E. (2005, December). A constructivist look at life roles. *The Career Development Quarterly,* 54(2), 138-149.

Brunning, F. (2007, Spring). Retirement: How one litigator has redefined the concept. *The Advocates' E-Brief, 18*(3) 21-22.

Campbell, C. & Ungar, M. (2004, Summer). Constructing a life that works: Part 1, blending postmodern family therapy and career counseling. *The Career Development Quarterly, 53,* 16-27.

Campbell, C. & Ungar, M. (2004, Summer). Constructing a life that works: Part 2, An approach to practice. *The Career Development Quarterly, 53,* 28-40.

Chandler, C.K., Holden, J. M. & Kolander, C.A. (1992, November/December). Counseling for spiritual wellness: Theory and practice. *Journal of Counseling & Development, 71*(2), 168-175.

Clemes, L.D. – see Treleaven, L.D. Clemes. (1999). Mid-life professional women envisage retirement: aspirations, attitudes and concerns. (Doctoral dissertation, University of Toronto, 1999) *Dissertation Abstracts International, A 60/08*, p. 2768.

Crose, R. Nicholas, D.R., Gobble, D.C. and Frank, B. (1992, November/December). Gender and wellness: A multidimensional systems model for counseling. *Journal of Counseling & Development, 71*(2), 149-156.

Daigneault, S.D. (1999, Fall). Constructing a Legacy: A third quarter task. *Career Planning and Adult Development Journal, 15*(3), 19-26.

Degges-White, S. & Myers, J.E. (2006, Fall). Women at midlife: An exploration of chronological age, subjective age, wellness and life satisfaction. *Adultspan Journal, 5*(2), 67-80.

Eichler, M. (1997) *Family shifts: Families, policies and gender equality.* Don Mills ON: Oxford University Press. p. 36.

Erdner, R.A. & Guy, R.F. (1990). *Career identification and women's attitudes to retirement. International Journal of Aging and Human Development, 30*(2), 129-139.

Francis, D. (1990). The significance of work friends in late life. *Journal of Aging Studies, 4*, 405-424.

Gabliani, V.I. (1993) Retirement decision-making in married professional women: An application of the theory of planned behavior (Doctoral dissertation, Washington University, 1993). *Dissertation Abstracts International, B 55/02*, p.589.

Greig, L.J.A (2006, November, 14). *Recent developments in Canadian laws affecting mature workers.* Presentation by Osler, Hoskin & Harcourt LLP at Summit on the Mature Workforce, Toronto, Canada.

Griggs, S. & Wright, S. (2001, Spring). Dowagers and dreams: Coaching women's later career stages. *Career Planning and Adult Development Journal, 17*(1), 13 – 26.

Growe, S.J. (2003, December 8). Uniting generations will improve the quality of life. *Toronto Star.* p. E7.

Growe, S.J. (2005, June 25). Graduation at long last. *The Globe and Mail,* p. F6.

Haid, R. & Williams, C. (1999, Fall). Counseling for the Third Quarter of Life. *Career Planning and Adult Development Journal, 15*(3), 5-8.

Hall, S.E. & Young, J.B. (1999, Fall). A model for coaching adults in late-life transitions. *Career Planning and Adult Development Journal, 15*(3), 27-32.

Harris, R. (2004, July 12). The Boomers' Golden Age. *Marketing Magazine. Rogers Media Inc.*

Herr, E.L. (1997, March). Super's life-span, life-space approach and its outlook for refinement. *The Career Development Quarterly, 45*(3), 238-246.

Hudson, F.M. (2001, Spring). Coaching "callings" throughout the adult life cycle. *Career Planning and Adult Development Journal, 17*(1), 7-12.

Hutching, P. & Elly Klimitz, B. (2004, December). Former surgeon teaching others in woodcarving craft. *Town Crier,* p.7.

Karp, D.A. (1989). The social construction of retirement among professionals 50-60 years old. *The Gerontologist, 29,* 750-760.

Kessler, P. (1999, Fall). (Early) retirement: An invitation

toward successful aging. *Career Planning and Adult Development Journal, 15*(3), 61-68.

Kimeldorf, M. (1999, Fall). Plan for some serious play. *Career Planning and Adult Development Journal, 15*(3) 99-105.

Kinjerski, V. & Skrypnek, B.J. (2008, June). Four paths to spirit at work: Journeys of personal meaning, fulfillment, well-being and transcendence through work. *The Career Development Quarterly, 56*(4), 319-329.

Korn/Ferry International & University of California, Los Angeles, Anderson Graduate School of Management, (1993). *Decade of the Executive Woman.* New York: Korn/Ferry International.

LaBauve, B.J. & Robinson, C. R. (1999, Spring). Adjusting to retirement: Considerations for counselors. *Adultspan Journal, 1*(1), 2-12.

Leider, R.(1999, Fall). Repacking your bags for the last third of life. *Career Planning and Adult Development Journal, 15(3),* 9-14.

Lippert, L. (1997). Women at mid-life: Implications for theories of women's adult development. *Journal of Counseling and Development, 76,* 16-22.

Maples, M.F. & Abney, P.C. (2006, Winter). Baby Boomers mature and gerontological counseling comes of age. *Journal of Counseling and Development, 84,* 3-9.

Marshall, K. & Ferrao, V. (August 2007). "Participation of older workers." Statistics Canada – PERSPECTIVES, Catalogue no. 75-001-XIE. p. 5

Moen, P., Erickson, W.A., Agarwal, M., Fields, V., Todd, L. (2000). *The Cornell retirement and well-being study: Final report.* Ithaca, NY: Bronfenbrenner Life Course Center, Cornell University.

Moen, P. et al. (2001). Couples' work/retirement transitions, gender, and marital quality. *Social Psychology Quarterly*, 64(1), 55-71.

Myers, J.E., Sweeney, T. J. & Witmer, M. (2000, Summer). The wheel of wellness counseling for wellness: A holistic model for treatment planning. *Journal of Counseling & Development*, 78, 251-266.

Niemela, P. & Lento, R. (1993). The significance of the 50th birthday for women's individuation. *Women and therapy*, 14, 117-127.

Owens, N.C. (1999, Fall). Grey hairs and rocking chairs? – Don't bet on it! Educating adults in the third quarter and beyond. *Career Planning and Adult Development Journal*, 15(3) 91-97.

Peavy, R.V. (1996). *Constructivist counseling: A participant guide.* Victoria, British Columbia, Canada: University of Victoria.

Penick, J.M. & Fallshore, M. (2005, Spring). Purpose and meaning in highly active seniors. *Adultspan Journal*, 4(1), 19-35.

Price-Bonham, S. & Johnson, C.K. (1982). Attitudes towards retirement: A comparison of professional and nonprofessional married women. In M. Szinovacz (Ed.), *Women's retirement.* (pp. 123-138). Beverly Hills, CA: Sage.

Pryor, R.G.L., Amundson, N.E. & Bright, J.E.H. (2008, June). Probabilities and possibilities: The strategic counseling implications of the chaos theory of careers. *The Career Development Quarterly*, 56(4) 309-318.

Robson, S.M., Hansson, R.O., Abalos, A., & Booth, M. (2006). *Journal of Career Development, 33*, 156-177.

Rollins, J. (2005, Aug.) Living a life of leisure: All work and no play? How leisure participation affects life satisfaction. *Counseling Today,* 10-11.

Savickas, M.L. (1997, March). Advancing life-span, life-space theory: Introduction to the special edition. *The Career Development Quarterly, 45*(3), 236-246.

Savickas, M.L. (1997, March). Career adaptability: An integrative construct for life-span, life-space theory. *The Career Development Quarterly, 45*(3), 247-259.

Savickas, M.L. (2003, September). Advancing the career counseling profession: Objectives and strategies for the next decade. *The Career Development Quarterly, 52*(1), 87-96.

Shmotkin, D. & Eyal, N. (2003, Summer). Psychological time in later life: Implications for counseling. *Journal of Counseling & Development, 81,* 259-267.

Simon-Rusinowitz, L., Wilson, L., Marks, L., Krach, C. & Welch, C. (1998). Reconfiguring retirement for baby boomers. *Journal of Mental Health Counseling, 15,* 106-116.

Snyder, B.A. (2005, Spring). Aging and spirituality: Reclaiming connection through story telling. *Adultspan Journal, 4*(1), 49-55.

Tien, H.L.S. (2007, December). Practice and research in career counseling and development – 2006. *The Career Development Quarterly, 56*(2), 98-140.

Tornstam, L. (1996) Gerotranscendence – a theory about maturing in old age. *Journal of Aging and Identity, 1,* 37-50.

Turcotte, M. & Schellenberg, G. (2007, Feb.). A portrait of seniors in Canada, 2006. Statistics Canada Catalogue no. 89-519.

Index

B

Balance, 3, 10, 15, 20, 22, 76, 77, 98
Barriers, 111, 118, 120
Boomers, baby-boomers, ix, 25, 26, 31, 38-41, 90, 144, 151
Brehony, K.A., 28, 134, 139
Brunning, F., 137, 146

C

Career, ix, x, 18, 20, 24, 27-36, 39, 51, 52, 53, 57, 59, 60, 67, 74, 81, 84, 87, 91, 93, 94, 97, 98, 113, 119, 122, 124, 125, 135, 137, 140, 146-151
Change, viii, ix, x, 3, 5, 15, 20, 21, 23, 26, 32, 34, 40, 41, 83, 87, 103, 111, 113, 122, 123-126, 129, 132, 138, 141, 145
Clemes, L.D., 133, 134, 147
Community, 13, 15, 18, 21, 22, 24, 32, 35, 36, 76, 78, 79, 86, 90, 99, 101, 102, 122, 124, 128
Connection, 11, 13, 14, 16, 18, 19, 32, 36, 37, 69, 84, 86, 87, 88, 92, 93, 100, 114, 143, 145, 151
Couples, see also relationships, 25, 28, 29, 35-38, 80, 86, 87, 135, 150
Courage, 37, 61, 111, 118, 119, 126
Creativity, 37, 61, 65, 139, 142
Csikszentmihalyi, M., 69, 137, 143

D

Dream, 58-67, 71, 74, 77, 86, 88, 98, 99, 101, 104, 106, 107, 112, 113, 115-117, 119, 120, 124, 127-129, 135, 144, 148
Dychtwald, K., 10, 40, 131, 136, 142

E

Eichler, M., 29, 135, 147
Entrepreneur, 85, 105

F

Family, 14, 25, 26, 28, 29, 30, 35, 36, 38, 39, 41, 54, 57, 66, 76, 77, 80, 86, 89, 90, 91, 94, 98, 114, 120, 122, 146
Fear, 10, 19, 58, 65, 106, 116, 123, 128, 141

Financial, 20, 29, 30, 35, 36, 40, 55, 57, 81, 85, 90, 94, 96, 99, 104, 113, 116
Finlayson, J., 35, 135, 142
Foot, D.K., 90, 131, 138, 142
Frankl, V.E., 19, 133, 139
Freidan, B., 20, 28, 133, 134, 139
Friends, 6, 14, 17, 36-39, 54, 76, 84, 87, 89, 90, 100, 120, 122, 128, 147

G

Gabliani, V.I., 34, 135, 147
Griggs, S., 30, 135, 148
Growe, S.J., 89, 134, 138, 148
Growth, 13, 14, 15, 20, 21, 22, 32, 47, 63, 67, 78, 84, 107, 123, 137

H

Haid, R., 40, 136, 148
Healing, 11, 17, 126, 132, 144, 145, 146
Hollis, J., 140
Hudson, F.M., 10, 107, 131, 133, 138, 140, 148

I

Intimacy, 14, 38, 63

J

Journaling, 6, 64, 115, 120, 121

K

Karp, R.A., 136, 148
Korn/Ferry International, 134, 149

L

Learning, 13, 14-15, 16, 38, 65, 79, 84, 85, 88, 89, 91, 93, 99, 102, 104, 106, 107, 112, 117, 120, 123, 126, 127, 128
Legacy, 13, 15-16, 48, 69, 85, 120, 147
Leisure, 17, 25, 32, 35, 41, 80, 91, 133, 151
Life chapter, 4, 74, 129
Life purpose, 13, 15, 22
Life stage, x, 24, 26, 35, 67
Longevity, 10, 13, 24, 33, 117, 145

Loss, 17, 18, 20, 31, 124, 128, 141, 145
Love, 15, 139, 141, 143

M

McLean, P.D., 140
Meditation, 11, 17, 19, 115, 121, 137, 143
Memory, 16, 145
Mid-life, viii, ix, x, 4, 16, 18, 28, 30, 35, 37, 38, 41, 45, 46, 60, 62, 67, 68, 75, 77, 81, 84, 87, 94, 127, 134, 136, 139, 144, 147, 149
Moen, P., 36, 133, 135, 136, 149, 150
Motivation, 17, 19, 107, 112, 115, 124

O

Opportunities, vii, viii, ix, x, 11, 12, 15, 19, 24, 27, 29, 30, 33, 60, 66, 79, 80, 81, 93, 94, 96, 102, 105, 106, 116, 123, 126, 127
Options, ix, 4, 5, 25, 29, 30, 31, 35, 38, 73-75, 77, 79, 81, 82, 83, 84, 90, 91, 93, 94, 95, 96, 102, 104, 106, 113, 118, 120

P

Part-time work, 11, 29, 30, 31, 33, 34, 41, 82, 91, 98, 100, 106
Personality, 46, 52, 53, 61, 62, 118, 125
Pioneers, ix, 4, 23-24, 27, 32, 36, 37, 134
Planning, xiii, 35, 67, 74, 92, 95, 101, 104, 105, 107, 117, 118, 133, 150
Possibilities, ix, 3, 4, 5, 15, 19, 23, 27, 47, 58, 63, 64, 74, 82, 96, 100, 115, 119, 122, 126, 127, 150
Purpose, 13, 15, 20, 22, 30, 32, 38, 57, 84, 85, 86, 93, 130, 139, 140, 150

R

Reality checking, 75, 95, 99, 101, 103, 117
Rebalancing, 5, 12, 24, 74, 75, 79
Reclaiming, 66, 67, 77, 123, 151
Reiner, S., 17, 133
Reinventing, 5, 23, 24, 62, 73, 75, 78, 79, 112, 142
Relationships, 3, 14, 18, 35, 37, 38, 47, 51, 54, 55, 61, 63, 84, 86, 87, 94, 100, 113
Relocating, 25, 78, 86, 90, 91, 97, 99
Renewing, 5, 10, 24, 73, 74, 75, 77, 78, 79, 115, 122, 128, 139

Retirement, viii, x, xiii, 4, 5, 20, 23, 24, 25, 26, 28, 29, 30, 31, 32, 33, 34, 35, 36, 37, 39, 40, 60, 67, 79, 81, 86, 87, 91, 100, 104, 113, 116, 121, 133, 134, 135, 136, 137, 142, 144, 146, 147, 148, 149, 150, 151
Roles, 20, 25, 34, 49, 51, 55, 86, 98, 105, 125, 146
Rollins, J., 17, 133, 151

S

Sheehy, G., 26, 38, 134, 136, 141
Simon-Rusinowitz. L., 136, 151
Singles, 28, 80
Spirituality, 13, 15, 18, 19, 22, 46, 63, 89, 92, 93, 131, 132, 139, 141, 143, 146, 147, 151
Statistics Canada, 26, 33, 131, 135, 142, 149, 151
Stress, 11, 55, 132, 144, 145
Support, 6, 20, 21, 22, 28, 49, 51, 90, 104, 122

T

Technology, ix, 16, 29, 38, 39, 40, 61, 124
Transition, x, 5, 18, 24, 31, 33, 36, 40, 45, 49, 56, 60, 63, 80, 84, 85, 96, 98, 101, 111, 112, 113, 121, 122-125, 126, 135, 138, 141, 148, 150
Travel, 15, 17, 32, 38, 39, 41, 60, 67, 77, 80, 84, 87, 88, 89, 91, 92, 93, 96, 100, 102, 104, 105, 129
Treleaven, L., see Clemes, 133, 134, 147
Trends, 26, 29, 35, 80, 134, 142

V

Values, 3, 13, 18, 30, 32, 35, 36, 46, 56, 62, 70, 77, 78, 80, 90, 91, 98, 99, 103, 107, 123
Vision, 26, 27, 96, 105, 141, 142
Volunteering, x, 30, 31, 32, 35, 39, 51, 77, 80, 82, 92, 96, 97, 98

W

Weil, A., M.D., 11, 70, 132, 137, 146
Well-being, 9-13, 14, 16, 17, 19, 20, 21, 22, 30, 39, 59, 75, 84, 91, 132, 133, 136, 137, 144, 145, 146, 149
Williams, C., 136, 148
Workplace, 23, 24, 26, 27, 28, 29, 35, 40, 94, 100, 134
Wright, S., 30, 135, 148

ABOUT THE AUTHOR

Lorraine Clemes, Ed.D. is the founder of Life Design Consultants, a firm specializing in helping individuals to get clear about, and successfully take, their best next steps. A respected career consultant, coach, and facilitator, Lorraine's proven process and insightful questions have helped individuals to discover their strengths, explore creative options and develop sound strategies for achieving what *really* matters most to them. Her impact has been described by clients as enlightening, practical and empowering.

Lorraine especially enjoys working with mid-life individuals as they decide "what's next?" or navigate a transition, and with people who are striving to achieve their career ambitions and a healthy balance in their lives. Her personal experiences and interest in well-being led her to develop two successful stress management audio-programs.

For several years she delivered leadership programs and provided consulting within one of Canada's largest financial institutions. The past twenty years she has been privileged to provide coaching services to people from a broad spectrum of organizations and this has contributed to her understanding of the challenges and opportunities that her clients encounter in today's dynamic workplace.

Lorraine's graduate education was in counseling psychology and workplace learning and change at the University of Toronto. Her doctoral research explored how mid-life professional women were starting to reinvent the concept of retirement and her coach training at The Hudson Institute of Santa Barbara focused on adult transitions and renewal.

www.lifedesignconsultants.com